ISBN 978-1-330-14149-6
PIBN 10035949

1 MONTH OF
FREE
READING

at

www.ForgottenBooks.com

By purchasing this book you are eligible for one month membership to ForgottenBooks.com, giving you unlimited access to our entire collection of over 700,000 titles via our web site and mobile apps.

To claim your free month visit:

www.forgottenbooks.com/free35949

English
Français
Deutsche
Italiano
Español
Português

www.forgottenbooks.com

Mythology Photography **Fiction**
Fishing Christianity **Art** Cooking
Essays Buddhism Freemasonry
Medicine **Biology** Music **Ancient**
Egypt Evolution Carpentry Physics
Dance Geology **Mathematics** Fitness
Shakespeare **Folklore** Yoga Marketing
Confidence Immortality Biographies
Poetry **Psychology** Witchcraft
Electronics Chemistry History **Law**
Accounting **Philosophy** Anthropology
Alchemy Drama Quantum Mechanics
Atheism Sexual Health **Ancient History**
Entrepreneurship Languages Sport
Paleontology Needlework Islam
Metaphysics Investment Archaeology
Parenting Statistics Criminology
Motivational

FIFTH. EDITION.

HARMONY SIMPLIFIED

A SIMPLE AND SYSTEMATIC EXPOSITION.

OF THE

PRINCIPLES OF HARMONY

DESIGNED NOT ONLY TO CULTIVATE

A THOROUGH KNOWLEDGE OF CHORD-CONSTRUCTION

BUT ALSO

TO PRACTICALLY APPLY THAT KNOWLEDGE

AND TO DEVELOP

THE PERCEPTIVE FACULTIES

BY

F. H. SHEPARD

AUTHOR OF "HOW TO MODULATE," "PIANO-TOUCH AND SCALES," AND "CHURCH-MUSIC AND CHOIR-TRAINING."

NEW YORK

G. SCHIRMER

35 UNION SQUARE

1900

PREFACE.

This little work offers no apology for its publication. It aims at the following distinct objects : — I. To treat the subjects of Scales, Keys, Signatures, and Intervals so thoroughly that the pupil will be prepared to understand with ease the principles of chord-construction.—II. To present the subject of Chord-Construction in such a manner that the pupil will be obliged to form all chords himself, thus deriving a practical knowledge of the subject.— III. To discard all arbitrary rules. Instead of blindly struggling with a mass of contradictory rules, the pupil is made acquainted with the original principles from which the rules are derived, and his judgment cultivated to apply them with discretion.—IV. The principles of the natural resolution of dissonances are shown, instead of giving the rules for the resolution of chords of the seventh. The pupil will apply these principles not only to chords of the seventh, but to all fundamental dissonances. — V. The chords of the Dominant Seventh, the Diminished Seventh, the Major and Minor Ninth, and the Italian, French and German Sixth, are shown to be but different forms of the same chord, with a perfectly uniform resolution, thus enormously reducing the difficulty of understanding these harmonies, and diminishing the complexity of the whole Harmonic System.—VI. The system of " Attendant " Chords will be found very helpful in understanding those chords which, though outside the key, evidently are closely related to some of its triads. It is also of much assistance in reducing the art of Modulation

to a condition in which it can be studied step by step.—
VII. After the regular course in chord-connection is completed, a supplementary course of study is outlined, in order to gain proficiency in practically using all the means of giving variety to a composition or improvisation. This proficiency is indispensable to young composers and organists, but it is usually allowed to develop itself, as nearly all manuals of Harmony stop at this point. To expect a pupil to be able to introduce Suspensions, Passing-notes, Sequences, Anticipations, etc., into his improvisations, or even into his compositions, after reading the explanation of them, is like explaining to a novice how the Piano is played, and then expecting him to be able to perform.—VIII. A course in the Development of the Perceptive Faculties is given, training the pupil to listen intelligently to music, to distinguish between the various chords, etc., and to write, in musical notation, what he hears.—
IX. A chapter on Musical Form is added, together with suggestions in regard to the Analysis of standard works.

Owing to the pressure of professional duties, as well as to the consciousness of his inability to improve on them the author has taken the exercises with figured basses chiefly from the "Manual of Harmony" by Jadassohn, and the "Manual of Harmony" by Richter, indicating the exercises of the former by the letter J., and those of the latter by R. These exercises are supplemented by others, designed for special purposes.

TABLE OF CONTENTS.

PART I.

SCALES: KEYS: INTERVALS.

SCALES AND KEYS.

INTERVALS.

PART II.

CHORDS.

TRIADS.

INVERSION OF TRIADS.

CHORD OF THE SEVENTH.

MODULATION.

PART III.

VARIETY OF STRUCTURE.

UNESSENTIAL NOTES.

MISCELLANEOUS SUBJECTS.

HARMONIZING MELODIES.

ANALYSIS AND FORM.

Note I. The student is urged to make frequent and persistent use of the keyboard for all appropriate exercises here given, for by this the practical efficiency of the study is greatly increased. Exercises in Scale, Interval, and Chord construction, in Chord connection, and Chord resolution, are suitable, but not the exercises in Part Writing.

Note II. Students using this volume for self-instruction, and teachers who desire a carefully graded system of Class Drill at the keyboard, are referred to the author's " Keyboard Harmony," which is designed to precede, or to be used in connection with the regular study of Harmony. This book will be issued early in 1901.

Note III. For use in Class Drill the " Keyboard Diagram," published separately, is of value, for by its use a large class may receive the same practical and thorough keyboard drill as the single individual at the piano.

PART I.

CHAPTER I.

Construction of the Major Scale.

1. A *Major Scale* is a succession of eight tones, placed at a distance of either a *Whole* or a *Half*-step apart.

A *Half-step* or *Semitone*, is the smallest interval formed upon the Piano-keyboard; that is, from any key to the next one, white or black; e. g., C to D♭: E to F: A♯ to B, etc.

A *Whole Step* is a step as large as two Half-steps; e. g., C to D: E to F♯: G♯ to A♯: B♭ to C.

2. The eight notes of a scale are called *Degrees* of the scale, and are numbered from the lowest, or Keynote, upward to the octave of the keynote.

5

3. Notice, when playing the scale of C on the Piano, that from the 3rd to the 4th degree, and from the 7th to the 8th, are *half*-steps, while between all the other degrees are *whole* steps. *This forms our rule for the construction of any Major scale,* (also called Diatonic* Major scale,) *without regard to the starting-place.* Therefore, we will write the succession of figures, indicating the position of the half-steps by the sign ⌣, thus making a *Formula*, or general pattern, by which we can construct a scale starting from *any* note; thus :—

1　2　3⌣4　5　6　7⌣8.　Briefly expressed for memorizing, this formula is as follows :—

    The *Half*-steps are from 3 to 4 and from 7 to 8.

    All other steps are *Whole* steps.

4. To illustrate this formula, let us begin on the note G, and, following the above rule, form a scale :—

G　A　B　C　D　E　F　G.　Let us examine this step
1　2　3⌣4　5　6　7⌣8.

by step, comparing the notes with the formula :—

1 to 2 should be a whole step, i. e., G to A — is right.
2 to 3 should be a whole step, i. e., A to B — is right.
3 to 4 should be a half-step, i. e., B to C — is right.
4 to 5 should be a whole step, i. e., C to D — is right.
5 to 6 should be a whole step, i. e., D to E — is right.
6 to 7 should be a whole step, i. e., E to F — is wrong, since E to F is only a *half*-step, where a *whole* step is required. To correct this, F♯ is used instead of F, giving the proper distance from 6. 7 to 8 should be a half-step,

---

* The word *Diatonic* means literally "through all the tones." Its applied meaning is, that one (and only one) note is to be written upon each degree of the staff. It will be seen later that the word is also used to refer to *scale-notes*, to distinguish them from notes altered by accidentals. (See § 44.)

i. e., F♯ to G — is right. (The F♯ really corrects two faults, as without it the step 7 to 8 would have been too great.) Expressed in notes with the formula, the corrected scale reads as follows :—

Fig. 1

In this way the pupil should test each note in the following exercises.

5. In constructing scales, observe the following points :

I. Do not write two notes upon the same degree of the staff; e. g., A and A♯.

II. Do not skip any letter; e. g., (The letter B is skipped.)

NOTE. The word Scale is derived from *Scala,* meaning "ladder." The lines and spaces are used *consecutively* to form a regular series of steps, ascending or descending. If two notes should be written upon one degree of the staff (e. g., I), it would be necessary to omit the note on the next degree (e. g., II) to make up for it. Such a method would make a very irregular looking scale or ladder; e. g.,

Fig. 2.

III. To avoid the errors mentioned in I and II the beginner should always first make a *skeleton,* or outline, of the desired scale, i. e., the notes only, without sharps or flats, writing the formula of figures underneath. Afterwards he may bring it to the required standard of steps and half-steps by using sharps or flats. For example :—

Fig. 3

The next step is to "write in" the sharps necessary to make the notes correspond with the formula. The process is as follows :—

1 to 2 should be a whole step; a whole step from F♯ is G♯: therefore, write a sharp before G.

2 to 3 should be a whole step; a whole step from G♯ is A♯: write a sharp before A.

3 to 4 should be a *half*-step; a half-step from A♯ is B— is right.

Proceed in this manner till the scale is completed, resulting as shown in Fig. 4.

Fig. 4.

Exercises.

6. Construct the Skeleton and Formula, and write Major scales starting from the following notes : C ; G ; D ; A ; E ; B ; F♯ ; C♯.

Double Sharps.

7. Write the scale of G♯ as above. N. B. It will be observed that the step 6 to 7, from E♯ a *whole* step upward, is not properly expressed by simply writing F♯, as that is only a *half*-step from E♯. It is here necessary to raise the F♯ *another* half-step, to make the required distance from E♯, which is done by using a *double* sharp, written x, giving

Exercises.

Write the scales of D♯, A♯, E♯, and B♯, using double sharps where necessary.

The Use of Flats.

8. Flats are introduced where without them notes would be a half-step too high. For example, in the scale starting upon F, (write it,) the interval from 3 to 4 is a whole step, while the formula requires a half-step.

This is rectified by the use of a flat before B.

Exercises.

Write the scales of F, B♭ E♭, A♭, D♭, G♭, and C♭.

Double Flats.

9. In the following scales, double flats, written ♭♭, will be required. From the foregoing, the pupil should be able to find the reasons without further explanation.

Exercises.

Write the scales of F♭, B♭♭, E♭♭, A♭♭, and D♭♭.

Advanced Course.

10. From a consideration of the above it will be seen, that in one sense there is but *one* Major scale. The so-called various scales, F, D, C♯, B♭, etc., are but *exact reproductions of each other*, varying only in pitch. The name of the scale, therefore, merely indicates the name of the starting-note or Keynote. There is a popular idea among Piano-pupils that the scale of C Major, having no black keys, is the one per-fect scale. But it will be at once seen that the Major scales are all alike in the manner of construction, the black keys upon the Piano simply serving to bring all the notes of the scale into proper relationship with each other, i. e., at the proper distance from each other. For exam-ple, it should not be said that there is a wide difference between the scale of C and the scale of D♭, because one has no flats and the other so many. Rather should it be said, that these five flats serve to make the two scales alike, by keeping the series of steps and half-steps absolutely the same.

Keys.

Regular Course.

11. After writing a few scales as above indicated, the

pupil will understand that the notes of the scale have a certain relationship with each other. The foundation or starting-point of each scale is termed the Keynote, and the group of tones composing the scale, considered collectively, is called a Key.

Signatures.

12. *Exercises.*—Returning to the exercises in §§6 and 8, the pupil will gather the sharps or flats used in constructing each scale, and place them in a group immediately after the clef, thus forming the Signature of the key.

Signatures are a *result* of this uniform construction of the scale, and not the cause or origin of the various keys.

Circle of Keys with Sharps.

13. In forming the key-signatures as above, notice :—

(*a.*) That each successive scale has one more sharp than the one before it; e. g., C has no sharps, G has one sharp, D two, A three, etc.

14. (*b.*) That the note on the 5th degree of one scale is used as the first note of the next scale; e. g.,

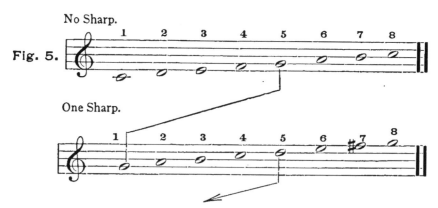

Fig. 5.

15. (*c.*) This succession continues till the note B♯ is reached. This note being the same as C natural, we may be said to have completed the Circle of Keys, starting from

C and continuing till the same note (though called B♯)
is reached.   This is called the Circle with Sharps.

16. (*d.*) The sharps or flats of a signature are always
written in the order in which they successively appear in
the Circle of Keys; e. g., F♯ being the first to appear, is
always written first,—at the left,—no matter how many
sharps there may be in the signature.   C♯, being second,
always comes next to F♯ in any signature.   Written in
order, and numbered, they appear as in Fig. 6.

Fig. 6.*

Notice, also, that if a certain signature has one sharp,
that sharp will be the one at the left in Fig. 6.   If a
signature has two sharps, they will be the two at the left
in Fig. 6.   And no matter how many there are, those at
the left will always be included.   To learn the order in
which the *flats* appear, observe the order of their entrance
in the illustrations and exercises in §§ 19–22.

17. (*e.*) It may be especially noticed, not only that
the note upon the 5th degree is used as a starting-point
for the succeeding new scale, but that the *last half* of
one scale (four notes) is used as the first half of the
next new one; e. g., Fig. 5. (See also §§ 32 and 45.)

18. (*f.*) But one note (or letter) is altered in passing
from one scale to the next in succession.   *This altered
note is always on the 7th degree*, and is shown by the
added sharp appearing in the Signature.**

---

* This order will be observed by reference to the entrance of each successive
new sharp in the Exercises, § 6.

** This fact may be used to find the Key indicated by any signature: The last
new sharp being always at the right in the signature, we may say that *the
right-hand sharp is always on the 7th degree of the scale.*   And, knowing the
7th degree, we may easily find the 8th degree or Keynote. (N. B. The octave
of the keynote is the same as the keynote itself.)

Circle of Keys with Flats; Circle of Fourths.

19. A Circle of Keys using a gradually increasing number of *flats*, can also be formed, by using the 4th degree of each scale as the starting-note (keynote) of the next one ; e. g.

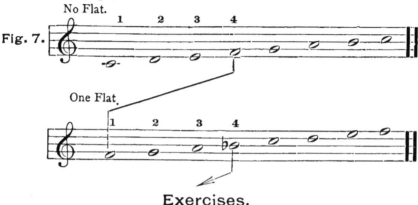

Fig. 7.

Exercises.

20. Write out the Circle of Keys with flats, using double flats where necessary.

21. It will be noticed that whereas in the Circle with sharps the last half of each scale forms the first half of the next, in flats this is reversed, the first half of one becoming the last half of the next. (To understand this, write it out in notes.) The pupil will further notice, that the added or new flat will appear each time upon the 4th degree.*

22. In the Circle of Keys with sharps, the 5th note of the scale is used as the Keynote of the following scale. In the Circle with flats, the 4th note is so used. Now, counting four notes of the scale upward reaches the same note as counting five notes downward.** Therefore, these circles are called the *Circle of Fifths*, the sharps counting

---

* Therefore, to recognize any key with flat signature, notice that the right-hand flat is on the fourth degree of the scale ; and to find the 1st degree or key-note, count downward from 4 to 1.

** In finding the fifth below, do not count 1, 2, 3, 4, 5 ; but, instead, count 5, 4, 3, 2, 1, remembering to keep the half-step between 4 and 3, in order to preserve the correct form in the new scale.

upward, i. e., by *ascending* Fifths, and the flats downward, i. e., by *descending* Fifths.

23. These circles may be represented as follows, the
figures opposite each key indicating the number of sharps
or flats in the signature :—

Fig. 8.	Fig. 9.
Read around to the right.	Read around to the left.

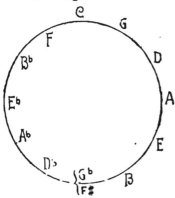

N. B.   In finding the above number of sharps or flats
in a signature, remember that a Double sharp counts the
same as two single sharps.

24. As the keys having more than six sharps or six
flats are unnecessarily complicated in notation, it is customary to use the sharp keys for the first half of the circle,
from C to F♯, and the flat keys to complete the round;
e. g., Fig. 10.

Fig. 10.
Read to right or left.

In this way the change is
usually made from F♯ to G♭,
or vice versa; though it *may*
be made at *any point in the
circle*, e. g., from G♯ to A♭,
from F♭ to E, etc., and is
called an *Enharmonic* change
of key.   See §78.

Advanced Course.

25. There is an interesting way of learning the *number of sharps* in a signature where there are more than six: It will be seen at a glance that the key of C has no sharps, and the key of C♯ has seven sharps. In other words, each of the seven notes has been raised by a sharp. Similarly, if the key of G has one sharp, the key of G♯ will have $1 + 7 = 8$, since each one of the notes in its scale must be raised to change the key from G to G♯. Similarly, the key of D having two sharps, the key of D♯ will have $2 + 7 = 9$. Similarly, the key of A having three sharps, the key of A♯ will have $3 + 7 = 10$. Therefore, to find how many sharps there are in a key when the Keynote is written with a sharp, simply add 7 to the number of sharps in the signature of the key of the *same letter* without the sharp.

26. The same principle applies to flat keys having more than six flats; e. g., B♭ has two flats; therefore B♭♭ will have $2 + 7 = 9$ flats.

27. Another interesting point in this connection may here be developed : —

In the Circles of Fifths in §§ 13–24, the circle began each time with the key of C. This is not at all necessary, it being quite as easy to begin upon *any other* note and complete the circle back to that note again, proceeding in either direction.

Let the pupil begin upon G♭ and form the circle by ascending fifths. This will decrease the number of flats by one each time till C is reached, after which sharps will appear and increase successively. Vice versa, a circle can be constructed beginning upon F♯ and progressing by *descending* fifths. Notice that in both cases the succession passes through the key of C and changes from flats to sharps, or vice versa, without altering the conditions in the least.

28. From this it will be seen that Flats and Sharps, in their relation to each other, are like degrees above and below Zero on the thermometer, sharps being above and flats below the zero-mark. Or they might be compared to Positive and Negative quantities in Algebra.

Exercises.

Form examples of the above-mentioned circles, starting in turn from C♯, D, D♯, E, F, F♯, G, G♯, A, A♯, and B, progressing first by *ascending* fifths, and afterward by descending fifths.

29. Resulting from the relationship of sharps and flats, keys are frequently compared with respect to their relative "sharpness," the key having the fewest flats or the most sharps being called the sharpest key. Or they may be placed in order, thus :—

Cb Gb Db Ab Eb Bb F C G D A E B F♯ C♯

7   6   5   4   3   2   1   0   1   2   3   4   5   6   7, and compared by saying

that one key is so many "*removes*" to the right (i. e., sharper) or left (1. e., flatter) from another key, counting through the key of C regardless of differences; e. g., G is two removes to the right from F, or B♭ is four removes to the left from D. (See Weitzmann's "Musical Theory," page 90.) In a similar way the notes themselves may be compared, saying that D is a sharper note than G, since its key is represented by one more sharp, etc. This point is further noticed in § 250.

Exercises.

Compare the sharpness of the following keys,— i. e., tell how many degrees or "removes" from the first to the second in each pair, and state which is the sharper of the two —

Keys of A and B; A and D ; B and F♯; A♭ and D ; B♭ and A♯; C and B♯; G♭ and A♭ ; D♭ and E♭ ; G♯ and A♭ ; F and G ; G and A ; A and B ; B and C.

Exercises.

Regular Course.

30. By means of the statements in foot-notes to §§ 18 and 21, the pupil should be able to recognize at sight any key from its signature :—

What keys are represented by the following signatures ?—

31. It is also desirable to know the number of sharps or flats in the signature of a given key, without reference to a table.

Exercises.

Give the number of sharps or flats in the signatures of the following keys: A, D♭, G, B♭, A♭, D, B, F♯, G♭, E♭, E.

N. B. If necessary to do so, write out each scale to find the number of sharps or flats.

Related Keys.

32. Keys having most notes in common are said to be *related* to each other. In the Circle of Fifths, each key is related particularly to the one before it, since one half of it is found in that scale; and also to the one following since the other half will be found in that one (see § 45), e. g., the key of C is related to the key of G; also to the key of F. This subject will be developed further. (See §§ 17 and 334.)

Exercises.

Name the two keys related to the key of B: of F♯: of D: of A♯: of E♭: of A: of G♭: E: D♯.

Facility in Distinguishing the Various Degrees of a Key by Number and by Name.

33. To thoroughly prepare himself for the subsequent chapters, the pupil should learn to recognize at a glance the various degrees of any scale, and indicate them by number or by name.

Exercises.

Placing any desired scale before the pupils (for example, the scale of B♭), the teacher should ask various questions like the following :—

Which degree of the scale is E♭? *Ans.* 4th degree.
Which degree of the scale is G? *Ans.* 6th degree.
Which degree of the scale is D? *Ans.* 3d degree.

This exercise should be carried through various keys, and continued till some proficiency has been gained. The exercise may be varied by such questions as the following :—

What is the 2nd degree in the scale of A major? *Ans.* B.

What is the 3rd degree in E major? *Ans.* G♯.

Specific Names.

(*To be learned.*)

34. Each Degree of the scale has also a Specific name, which is often used instead of the number as follows :—

1st degree, **Tonic.**

2d degree, **Supertonic.**

3d degree, **Mediant.** (Meaning midway between Tonic and Dominant.)

4th degree, **Subdominant.**

5th degree, **Dominant.**

6th degree, **Submediant.** (Midway between Tonic and Sub-dominant, when the latter is written *below* the former.)

7th degree, **Subtonic or Leading-Tone.**

8th degree, **Octave or Tonic.**

Exercises.

Apply test-questions, as shown in § 33.

Notice that the prefix " Sub " means " below," and " Super," " above :" e. g., Supertonic means the degree above the Tonic, and Subtonic the degree below the Tonic.

The Tonic, Dominant, Subdominant, and Leading-note are especially important to know, and the pupil *should be able to find them without hesitation in any key.*

The Minor Scale.

35. It was noticed that in the Major Scale the half-steps occur from 3 to 4, and from 7 to 8. The Minor Scale is formed by placing the half-steps between 2 and 3, 5 and 6, 7 and 8.

Fig. 11.

This is called the *Harmonic* Minor Scale, to distinguish it from the *Melodic* Minor Scale, which has a different and irregular arrangement of the half-steps, as shown in Figure 12.   (See also § 46.)

Fig. 12.

36. The Harmonic Minor Scale is the basis of the chords in the Minor Mode,* while the Melodic Minor Scale is generally used in melodies.   It may be considered as a " free" form of the Harmonic scale, made necessary by the fact that the interval of 1½ steps from 6 to 7 in the Harmonic Minor Scale (see Fig. 11) is rather unmelodious, though not unmusical.

37. From the foregoing comparison of the Major and Minor scales, the pupil will realize that *the character of a scale depends upon the position of the half-steps.*

Exercises.

38. Form Harmonic Minor scales, and write the figures under each note as shown in Fig. 11, starting from the following notes: A, E, B, F♯, C♯, G♯, D♯, D, G, C, F, B♭, E♭, A♭, D♭.

Relative Minor.

39. Every Major scale has what is called its "Relative Minor," which is the Minor scale having most notes in common with it, and having the *same signature.*   This Relative Minor is always founded (has its keynote, or Tonic) on the *sixth degree of the Major scale.*   Thus,

---

* The words " Major Mode" and " Minor Mode" are terms used when we do not refer to any particular key, but wish to speak of the character of Major or Minor in a general way.

the sixth degree in the scale of C is A; therefore, the Relative Minor of C Major is the scale (or key) of A Minor. (In finding a relative minor, it may be easier for the pupil to look for the keynote 1½ steps below rather than the sixth above, the result being the same.)

Exercises.

Find the Relative Minor (and write the proper signature) of C Major; of G, D, A, E, and B Major; of F, B♭, E♭, A♭, D♭ Major.

40. Correlatively, each Minor has its Relative Major, which is found on the third degree of the Minor scale. For example, the relative major of A Minor is C Major. In other words, A Minor is the relative Minor of C Major; and C Major is the relative Major of A Minor.

Exercises.

Find the Relative Majors of the following Minor scales: A, E, B, F♯, C♯, G♯, D♯, D, G, C, F, B♭, E♭, A♭, D♭.

Signatures in Minor.

41. The pupil will notice that the Relative Minor of any Major scale has the same notes as the latter, excepting the seventh degree, which is raised by an accidental. For example, A Minor has the same notes as C Major excepting the G♯. This accidental raising of the seventh degree is caused by the fact that the seventh degree, or "Leading-tone," should be only a half-step distant from the Tonic. (See § 46.)

In collecting the sharps or flats to form the signature of a minor key, this fact should be considered :— *The accidental found before the seventh degree does not belong to the signature.*

Exercises.

Write the signatures of the following Minor keys, proceeding as directed in § 12 : A, E, B, F♯, C♯, G♯, D♯, D, G, C, F, B♭, E♭.

The Circle of Keys in Minor.

42. The Circle of Fifths can be made with Minor keys as well as with Major.

Exercises.

(*a.*) Form the Circle with sharps, beginning with the key of A Minor.

(*b.*) Form the Circle with flats, beginning with the key of A Minor.

(*c.*) Form the Circle beginning upon various other notes.

The Chromatic Scale.

43. When the half-steps lying between the notes of the Diatonic scales are included, thus producing a scale of half-steps exclusively, it is called a Chromatic scale. It is customary to use sharps in writing the intermediate half-steps in an ascending chromatic scale, and flats in the descending scale ; e. g.,

Fig. 18.

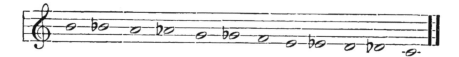

Chromatic Alteration.

44. When a note is raised or lowered a half-step by

an accidental, consequently *without changing its position upon the staff*, it is said to be chromatically altered;

e. g.,

A *Chromatic* Half-Step is one expressed upon *one* degree of the staff; e. g., A — A♯.

A *Diatonic* Half-Step is one expressed upon *two* degrees of the staff; e. g., A — B♭.

In general, a Diatonic progression is one where the *letter is changed* in the succession of notes; and a Chromatic progression is one where the *letter is not changed*, but altered by the use of an accidental.

At the close of each chapter the pupil should make a synopsis of the principal facts contained therein, classifying and arranging them in order. The following table is intended to assist the pupil in this.

Synopsis of Chapter I.

Scales:

Major:
- Formula :— Half-steps 3–4 and 7–8.
- Keys.
- Signatures.
- Circle of Fifths : { Ascending. / Descending. }
- Relative Keys : { Fifth above, or Dominant. / Fifth below, or Subdominant. / Relative Minor. }
- Specific Names.
- Major scales all alike.

Minor:
- Formula : { Harmonic; Half-steps, 2–3, 5–6, 7–8. / Melodic; Half-steps, up, 2–3, 7–8 : down, 6–5, 3–2. }
- Relative Major.
- Signatures : { Same as Relative Major. / Omit sign of raised Leading-note. }
- Leading-note raised by an accidental.

Chromatic: { Position of half-steps. / Notation. }

Historical.

45. The Modern Scale is a gradual development from the ancient Greek Modes, in which the semitones occupied varying places in the scale, according to the mode. See Grove's "Dictionary of Music;" Vol. II, p. 341, and Baker's "New Dictionary of Musical Terms;" p. 88 *et seq.* The Major Scale may be considered as composed of two Tetrachords,* placed one above another; e. g.,

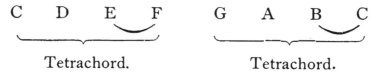

C   D   E   F   G   A   B   C

Tetrachord.   Tetrachord.

Until the 13th century, the use and influence of the semitones in Music were not fully realized; therefore, in the music previous to that time, we find (according to modern standards) a lack of Tonal feeling, or sense of being in some particular key.   In the time of Palestrina it became customary to *sing* the seventh degree as if it were only a half-step from the eighth, although this was contrary to the notation, showing the need of something beyond the scales then in use.

In the seventeenth century the modern scale began to displace the Gregorian Modes; the sharps and flats, instead of being dispersed through the composition or left to the discretion of the performer, were gathered to gether to form the signature; the dividing lines between the keys were thus more distinctly marked; and Modern Music, as opposed to the Ancient Modes, soon made a distinct place for itself.

46. The oldest form of the Minor scale was as shown in Fig. 14.

---

* A Tetrachord is a scale of four notes, having one half-step.   Tetrachords belonged to the musical system of the ancient Greeks.

Fig. 14.

As the feeling of Tonality developed, a "Leading-note" was demanded which should point more decidedly toward the Keynote, and thus impart a greater feeling of satisfaction when the final chord was reached.* Thus the 7th degree of the scale was raised by an accidental, giving the form as in Fig. 15, which is seen to be our present Harmonic Minor scale.

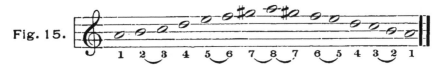

Fig. 15.

This form leaves an interval of $1\frac{1}{2}$ steps between the 6th and 7th degrees; and for the sake of a smoother effect it became customary to raise the 6th degree also a half-step, where the harmony would allow it, giving the form shown at (a), Fig. 16, which is our present Melodic Minor scale.

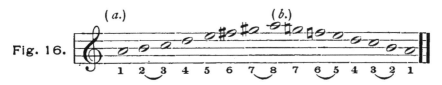

Fig. 16.

A "Leading-note" being unnecessary in a descending scale, the two notes raised by accidentals in the

* The need of a " Leading-note " to give the feeling of satisfaction when the final chord is reached, is shown by comparing (*a*) and (*b*) in Fig. 17.

Fig. 17.

ascending scale are usually restored in the descending scale (*b*), Fig. 16. This gives the complete Melodic minor scale as used at the present day.

Exercises in Musical Dictation, for the Development of the Perceptive Faculties.

47. If we would rightly understand Music, it is indispensable that we become able to recognize what we hear, just as we recognize printed words upon first sight.

The reason so few have the faculty of listening intelligently, is not that it is difficult, but because little or no attention has been paid to this most important subject. Briefly summed up, the steps of the process of development consist in gaining the power:

1. To distinguish the various notes of the scale.
2. To distinguish Intervals.
3. To distinguish the Major from the Minor Mode.
4. To distinguish Chords and their inversions, and to realize their position in the key.
5. To trace simple Modulations.
6. To distinguish the Divisions of Time, Rhythm, etc.
7. To note the various features of Form, learning to recognize Motives, Themes, succession of keys, Periods, and the general plan of construction.
8. To be able to express all of the above in Musical Notation.*

By taking this study step by step, and in connection with the study of Harmony, there will be added interest in the latter by reason of the ability to apply each point as soon as learned. There will also be a deeper and more practical comprehension of Harmony, and a more intelligent knowledge of Music as an Art and a Science.

To Distinguish Notes of the Scale.

48. (*a.*) The best and only really successful manner of teaching the notes of the scale and how to distinguish them, is through the medium of the voice. The foundation of the musical perceptions lies in the possession of a "working" knowledge of the Major scale. The first

---

* The above represents the complete process, facility in all of which is attained only by gifted minds. But a moderate degree of proficiency is within reach of any one possessed of ordinary perseverance.

step is therefore to thoroughly practise singing the major scale, using the syllables Doh, Ray, Me, Fah, Soh, Lah, Te, Doh¹.* This should be continued till the pupils can skip from any degree to any other, and can also recognize the same when sung or played by the teacher.

(*b.*) In connection with the above, the teacher should sing, or play the ascending and descending scale, while the class, provided with a book of score-paper, write each note as it is sung. During this exercise (of writing, or *musical dictation*) the teacher should frequently ask, " What was the last note sung ?" requiring as an answer the name of the syllable, Doh, Ray, etc.

49. (*c.*) The scale may now be broken up ; for example, going up a few notes and coming down part way ; then going up a little further, etc., taking care to have all the progressions diatonic, — i. e., no skips, and no notes altered by accidentals. (The pupils should write these notes as sung or played.)

(*d.*) Afterward, simple skips (3ds, 4ths, and 5ths) may be interspersed, always keeping enough of the diatonic progression to retain the feeling of tonality, and taking care to increase the difficulty very gradually.

These exercises must be practised thoroughly, in order to lay the foundation for the more difficult subsequent studies. The keys in which these dictation-exercises are written, should be frequently changed during a lesson, that all keys may become familiar. It is not necessary that the teacher should play in a different key when the change is made. He may simply say, striking any note on the Piano : " This note is Doh : write in the key of ——," After a time he may say : " Now write in the key of ——' mentioning any key he may desire. Thus the pupils will become able to express themselves in one key as easily as in another, and will realize that the great point is the *relationship* of the sounds rather than the actual notes.

50. Although the ability to sing any succession of tones may not appear very requisite for the first exercises, it will be found in the subsequent studies in recognizing chords, modulations, etc., that the highest possible development of this power is of great advantage. Therefore, the practice of singing the scale and skipping about in it should be continued for some time. A diagram like Fig. 18, written on a wall-chart, is best for the first practice.

---

*The use of syllables is helpful in establishing the relationship of the various notes to each other.

Fig. 18.

Fah¹

Me¹

Ray¹

DOH¹

TE

LAH

SOH

FAH

ME

RAY

DOH

Te₁

Lah₁

Soh₁

51. Besides practice in singing different tones, the pupil should be exercised in *thinking* how a succession of notes would sound. For example, taking a short succession like

Fig. 19.

the pupil should, by remembering the syllabic names of the notes and the sounds connected with those names, try to think how the passage would sound, afterward comparing with the effect when sung or played.

52. While exercising the pupil on Pitch, studies in Rhythm should be given, by means of notes of various lengths, successions of notes with rhythmic flow, etc. Rests should also be introduced. The inexperienced will find material for such exercises in any book on Sight-singing or Musical Dictation.

CHAPTER II.

INTERVALS.

53. An Interval in Music is like an interval anywhere else, — it is an expression of *distance* between two things. Consequently, it may be defined as the distance, or *difference in pitch*, between two given tones.*

54. An Interval may be formed by two notes, either sounded together, or in succession.—

Advanced Course.

* The word Interval may also mean the relationship of two notes in respect to pitch; or the *effect* produced by the two notes sounding together or in succession.

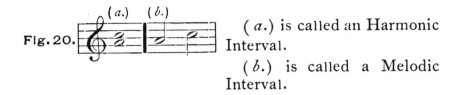

Fig. 20.

(*a.*) is called an Harmonic Interval.

(*b.*) is called a Melodic Interval.

General Names of Intervals.

55. An Interval is named according to the number of degrees of the scale included in its extent.

Thus, the Interval from C to D* is called a 2nd, because two Degrees of the scale are concerned in its production. Similarly, from C to E is a 3rd, from C to F a 4th, from E to B a 5th, etc.

56. To determine the name of an interval, count the degrees, including those upon which the notes of the interval stand (i. e., including extremes). For example, in determining the name of ▦, count the degrees upon which C and A stand, as well as those lying between, giving the total of six; therefore, the interval in question must be a 6th. N. B. Unless otherwise indicated, intervals are usually counted from the lower note upward.

Table of Intervals.

Fig. 21.

| Unison or Prime.** | 2d. | 3d. | 4th. | 5th. | 6th. | 7th. | 8th. | 9th. | 10th. |

---

* The *lower* note of an interval or chord is always mentioned first.

** When two voices sound the same note, there is no difference in pitch, and therefore no interval between them. Consequently, the Unison cannot strictly be called an interval.

Exercises.*

57. (*a.*) Form tables similar to the above, starting from the notes D, F, E, G, B, and A (all in the key of C).

(*b.*) Form similar tables in the keys of G, F, D, B♭, etc. .

(*c.*) Write all the Seconds in the key of G ; e. g.,

Fig. 22. 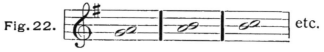 etc.

Write all the Thirds in the key of F.

Write all the Fourths, Fifths, Sixths, Sevenths and Octaves in the key of E ; in the key of B♭ ; A ; D♭ ; F♯.

Specific Names of Intervals.

58. Intervals are of various kinds, the names of which fairly express their meaning, as follows :—

Major: ⎱ ** The *normal or standard of measure-*
Perfect: ⎰ *ment.* The difference between the two will be explained in §§ 73 and 76.

Minor : meaning " less " by a semitone than Major.

Diminished: meaning still less, or less by a semitone than Minor or Perfect.

Augmented : meaning increased, or greater by a semitone than Major or Perfect.

The Standard of Measurement.

59. Consider the scale of C upon the keyboard. **From C to any other degree of the scale of C, or from C to any white key upon the Piano, is a Major or Perfect, i. e., a Normal, interval.**

(For example, see Fig. 21. All the intervals there

---

* Pupils are liable to make mistakes when counting an interval upon the keyboard ; but when written, by counting the lines or spaces upon which the notes stand and all the intervening lines and spaces, mistakes become impossible.

** For the present the pupil need only know that Unisons, Fourths, Fifths, and Octaves may be Perfect, but not Major. (Some theorists call the Perfect intervals *Perfect Major*, to distinguish them from those which are simply Major.)

given are Major or Perfect.)   This gives us a practical *standard of measurement by which we can measure any interval;* for, as we have seen in the above definitions, a Minor interval is a semitone smaller than a Major, an Augmented a semitone larger than a Major, etc.

60. The difference between the various kinds of intervals is illustrated by the following, from Eugene Thayer:—'Let us take a pair of hand-bellows, and allowing them to take their natural position, find them to be nearly wide open—the handles well apart.   Let this position represent the Major interval.   If the upper handle be pressed down a little, the distance between the two handles (or the interval) is lessened:,—this corresponds to the Minor interval.   If we now raise the lower handle pressing them still nearer together, the distance (interval) is again decreased, representing a Diminished interval. Again, letting the handles spring back to their original (normal) position, representing the Major interval, if we raise the upper handle, or depress the lower one, we increase the distance between them, thus representing an Augmented interval.'

61. It is not the mere elevation or depression of the notes that changes an interval, but the fact that the tones are either separated further from each other, or are brought nearer together; i. e., the *distance* is changed.

62. Let us make a practical application of the above.

We found in § 56, that from C to A (counting upward) is a Sixth; and, according to § 59 and foot-note, it is a Major Sixth : .

Let us apply some of the changes mentioned in § 58 to this.   Lowering the upper note a semitone, we have , which, being a semitone less than the Major Sixth, is called a Minor Sixth.

Again, taking this Minor Sixth, by again decreasing

the distance between the notes, this time raising the lower note by prefixing a sharp, we obtain a Diminished Sixth :* .

Again, returning to the Major Sixth as a starting-place, if the upper note be raised a half-step, the distance between the two notes will be increased forming an Augmented Sixth :

Exercises.

Name each of the following intervals.

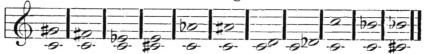

Exact Measurement of Intervals.

63. An interval can be exactly measured, and its Specific name placed beyond doubt by counting the number of *Half-Steps* contained in it (just as we counted the number of *degrees* to obtain the General name). For example, from C to A is a 6th. Counting the number of half-steps, we find it has nine. Therefore, as our Standard Sixth contains nine half-steps, *any other Major sixth*, without regard to its position, *must have the same number of half-steps.* According to § 58, an Augmented Sixth must have one half-step more, or ten half-steps : and a Minor Sixth one half-step less, or eight half-steps. In this way we may compare any interval with the Standard of Measurement, and learn whether it is Major, Minor, Diminished, or Augmented.

64. As no interval is commonly used in more than three of these forms, a table is subjoined, showing them in order as generally used.

---

*The interval of the Diminished 6th is not commonly used (see Table, §64). but it is useful here for illustration.

Table of Intervals.

Showing the number of *half*-steps in any interval.

[For reference ;— not to be memorized.*]

	Diminished.	Minor.	Perfect.	Major.	Augmented.
Primes:			o		1
Seconds:				2	^
Thirds:	2			4	
Fourths:	4		5		6
Fifths:	6		7		8
Sixths:		8		9	10
Sevenths:	9	10		11	
Octaves:	11		12	—	—
Ninths:		13		14	15

65. In working out the following exercises, the pupil should first find the note for the General name of the interval as shown in § 56, afterward adding any sharps or flats necessary to bring it into correspondence with the requirements of the Specific name. For example, "What is the Major Sixth from E?" Process:— Beginning to count with the note E, the sixth count will bring us to C; therefore, a Sixth from E must be C; C is thus the *General* name for the desired interval. Next, a Major Sixth must have (refer to the standard of measurement) nine half-steps: as there are but eight half-steps from E to C, it is evident that the latter must be raised by a sharp, giving, for the Major Sixth, C♯.

Advanced Course.

66. The standard of measurement, § 59, showed the intervals from the note C to every other note in the scale of C to be "Normal" intervals. In a similar way, from the *Keynote* of any other key *to any note of that scale* would be also a "Normal" interval, e. g., from A♭ to any

---

* It is unnecessary to memorize this table, as the pupil can easily find the number of half-steps in a given interval by the use of the principles shown in § 63.

note in the scale of A♭ would be just as "normal" as from C to any note in the scale of C. Therefore, instead of counting the half-steps in naming or forming a specific interval, the practised musician would think, "What is the 'Normal' interval?" counting from any given note (by transferring his thought for the instant to the key of that given note), and would raise or lower that normal note to obtain the required interval. For example: What is the Augmented Sixth from F♯? Process:—If we were in the key of F♯, the Normal Sixth would be found by counting up to the 6th degree of the scale, giving the note D♯. (Having found the desired interval, do not think further in the key of F♯.) As the required Augmented Sixth is a half-step greater than the Normal, the D♯ must be raised another half-step, giving the note D✕ (double sharp).

Regular Course.

67. Remember that the *General* name is obtained by counting the *degrees* of the scale, while the *Specific* name is found by counting the *half-steps*. Therefore, the use of *sharps or flats can never change the General name* of an interval;—a Sixth remains a Sixth even if there are several sharps or flats prefixed. The *kind* of Sixth it would be is quite a d.fferent question, coming under the head of *Specific* name.

Exercises.

68. (*a*) Form a Major Sixth from each of the following notes, counting upward:—D, E, F♯, B, A, B♭, A♭, D♭, A♯, G, E♭, G♭, C♭, G♯, C♯, F♭, B♯, etc.

(*b*.) From the same notes, form Major Thirds, Minor Thirds, Minor Sevenths, Diminished Sevenths, and Augmented Fourths.

Extended Intervals.

69. As an octave above any note is considered a repetition of that note and bears the same name, so intervals (with the exception of the Ninth), if they extend over

more than an octave, are considered as repetitions of the smaller intervals formed by the same notes an octave

nearer together. Thus : , which is an interval

of an Eleventh, is considered as an extension of

which is a Fourth. Therefore, in finding intervals, the notes should be brought within the compass of an octave.

Exercises.

Name the following intervals, lowering the upper note, or raising the lower, one or two octaves:

The interval of a Ninth is usually not contracted in this way, as the chord of the Ninth requires that interval to be nine degrees from the root. See Chapter VIII.

Inversion of Intervals.

70. By Inversion of Intervals is meant that the notes change their relative positions;—the upper one, by being lowered an octave (retaining its original name), becoming lower than the other; or, the lower one, by being raised an octave, becoming higher than its fellow. Thus, the interval at (*a*) in the accompanying figure becomes like (*b*) by lowering the upper note, and like (*c*) by raising the lower one, which is the same thing as (*b*), but an octave higher.

Exercises.

Invert the following (*a*) by lowering the upper note one octave; (*b*) by raising the lower note.

71. Subjoined is a Table showing a few intervals inverted. The lower staff shows the result of inverting the intervals contained in the upper staff. Notice that in the tables the inversions are produced by raising the lower note one octave. It would have been quite as easy to lower the upper notes one octave, writing the inversions in the Bass clef. The quarter-notes in the lower staff show the notes which have been raised an octave.

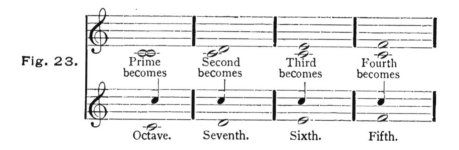

Fig. 23.

Prime becomes / Octave. Second becomes / Seventh. Third becomes / Sixth. Fourth becomes / Fifth.

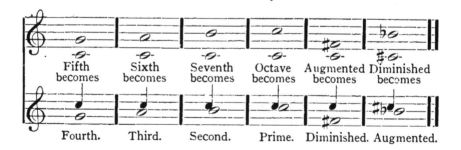

Fifth becomes / Fourth. Sixth becomes / Third. Seventh becomes / Second. Octave becomes / Prime. Augmented becomes / Diminished. Diminished becomes / Augmented.

72. From the above let us notice the following :—
(*a.*) To learn what will be the inversion of an interval

(that is, the interval which will result by inverting), subtract the number of the interval from 9, and the resul⸳ will be the interval produced by the inversion. For ex· ample, what would the interval of a Sixth become by inversion ? Process : $9 - 6 = 3$; therefore, a Sixth, when inverted, becomes a Third. (See p. 42, Addendum.)

The following table shows the fact still more clearly : —

From	9	9	9	9	9	9	9	9
Subtract	1	2	3	4	5	6	7	8
Result	8	7	6	5	4	3	2	1

From the first table (Fig. 23) we notice also :—

73. (*b*.) By inversion { Major intervals become Minor.
By inversion { Minor intervals become Major.

By inversion { Augmented intervals become Diminished.

By inversion { Diminished intervals become Augmented.

By inversion { Perfect intervals remain Perfect (and therefore Normal).

This pecularity of the Perfect intervals renders it necessary to class them differently from the Major, though in practical Harmony this distinction does not affect their use. A further difference between Major and Perfect intervals appears in § 76.

Exercises.

74. (*a*.) Find the Perfect intervals in Fig. 21. (There are four.)

(*b*.) From the note D form a series similar to Fig. 21, and invert each interval as shown in Fig. 23.

(*c*.) Write examples of Diminished and Augmented intervals, and invert them. To learn what Diminished and Augmented intervals are in use, the pupil may refer to the Table in § 64.

Consonant and Dissonant Intervals.

75. In the preceding paragraphs, intervals were classed according to the number of half-steps contained. They are also classed, according to their musical effect, as :—

(*a.*) *Consonant*, meaning those intervals upon which it is agreeable to pause, and which do not need to be followed by another interval to produce a pleasant effect ; and

(*b.*) *Dissonant*, or those which are not satisfactory to dwell upon, or to use in the final chord of any composition.

Consonances are further divided into *Perfect* and *Imperfect Consonances*, with reference to the *degree* of concord, as follows :—

Consonances.
  Perfect :
    All Perfect intervals, viz.,
    Perfect Prime (or Unison),
    Perfect Octave
    Perfect Fourth,
    Perfect Fifth.
  Imperfect :
    Major Thirds and Sixths.
    Minor Thirds and Sixths.

Dissonances.
  Seconds and Sevenths, together with all augmented and diminished intervals ; i. e., all intervals other than the Perfect intervals and Major and Minor Thirds and Sixths.

Exercises.

The pupil will refer to all the previous exercises and illustrations in this chapter, particularly to the Table in § 64, and mark each interval as Perfect or Imperfect Consonance or Dissonance.

76. A further difference between Major and Perfect intervals appears at this place. When a Major interval is decreased by a semitone (see § 62), it becomes a Minor interval, which is, however, just as " consonant " as the Major interval ; i. e., it still belongs to the " Consonant " intervals, as shown in the above table : whereas, if a Perfect interval be decreased by a semitone, it at once loses its characteristic of being " Consonant " and be-

comes a " Dissonant " interval. For example, is a Perfect Fifth. If we lower the upper note a semitone, the result is , which is a Diminished Fifth and a Dissonance. Thus we see that a Major interval can be made less (Minor) *without changing its classification* of " Consonant " ; while a Perfect interval *cannot* preserve its original classification when thus altered.*

Confusion of Terms.

77. There is much confusion in the terms used in connection with the Theory of Music. The pupil should therefore carefully notice to what each term refers. A few examples are given below of the various meanings of certain words :—

Degree may refer to the various steps of the Scale.

Degree may also refer to the lines and spaces of the staff.

Steps may refer to the various degrees of the Scale.

---

* The word " Perfect " conveys but little meaning, as these intervals are perfect only in respect to their quality of remaining " Normal " when inverted, while Major intervals do not. A more descriptive name might be " *Sensitive*" interval, as such an interval cannot be changed in any manner without producing a dissonance.

Steps and *Half-Steps* also to the distance between tones.

Tones and *Semitones* may refer to the distance be tween tones.

Tones may also refer to sounds, regardless of distance from other sounds.*

Interval refers to distance between tones.

Interval sometimes refers to the steps of the scale.

The names of the *Degrees of the Scale* (as Fifth degree, Third degree, etc.), are liable to be confused with the *Intervals of the same name:* therefore be careful to say whether you mean Degree or Interval.

Definitions.

78. *Diatonic Intervals.* The word Diatonic refers to the scale; a Diatonic interval would be, therefore, an interval formed by two notes of the scale without sharps or flats other than those indicated by the signature.

Chromatic Intervals. The word Chromatic in Music refers to the half-steps lying between the notes of the scale, and which are produced by the use of accidental sharps, flats, or naturals, to change the diatonic tones. A Chromatic interval, then, would mean one where at least one of the notes has an accidental sharp, flat, or natural before it.

N. B. A Half-step can be either Chromatic or Diatonic; e. g., from C to C♯ is a Chromatic half-step, because only one note (C) is concerned in the interval. (See § 44.) But if C♯ is called D♭, the half-step becomes Diatonic, because two notes (or two degrees on the staff) are concerned.

---

* The words *Note* and *Tone* are often used interchangeably, though a tone is properly a sound, and a note is a character to represent a sound to the eye.

Enharmonic. This word refers to the notation only;* when the same tone is expressed in two different ways, there is said to be an Enharmonic Change; e. g., A♭ when changed to G♯ is said to be enharmonically written, because the name has been changed while the tone remains the same. (See foot-note, and § 24.)

This chapter should *always* be studied twice (repeated very carefully) before proceeding, as it is impossible to understand the *full meaning* of the first part before the last part has been studied.

Synopsis.

79. Before proceeding, the pupil *should not fail to write a synopsis* of the chapter as suggested at the close of Chapter I, and endeavor to gain an orderly view of the subject. Failure to do this is often the cause of very confused ideas in regard to Harmony.

Historical.

80. The beginning of Music was Melody, everything being in unison and without accompaniment. In some MSS. of the 10th century, examples of church-music are found, progressing at the regular interval of a Fourth. The meaning of this has been disputed, some claiming that it was intended to be sung in unison and then repeated a Fourth higher, while others think the two parts were to be sung together, the effect of which would be disagreeable to modern ears.

At about this time a " Drone Bass " was sometimes used —i. e., a Bass continuing upon one note regardless of the melody. In this way various intervals, such as Fourths, Fifths, and Sixths, were necessarily, though quite accidentally, formed. Soon afterward (11th century) it was·

---

* Advanced students of theory may know that Enharmonic intervals have a *very slight* difference in pitch ; e. g., G♯ has a few vibrations more per second than A♭, though the Piano does not show it.

discovered that two complete and independent melodies might be sung together and produce a pleasant effect. From this discovery came Counterpoint, and before the close of the 14th century music was written in four parts, though little was known of the effects of harmony. At this period the controlling principle was to invent several melodies which would not conflict when sung together, rather than to study the effect of the combination of three or four tones forming a chord. Consequently, at this time, till the close of the 14th century, the *harmonic* effects were *accidental* rather than studied.

The Perceptive Faculties.

(Continued from page 24.)

Intervals.

81. The perception of intervals, though more difficult than of single tones, need not cause any especial trouble if properly presented, and if the first steps have been thorough. It is probable that the student will advance more rapidly in Theory than in the development of the perceptions. Do not try to make the two keep exact pace, though in explaining each chapter, the ear as well as the eye and the understanding should be actively interested.

Process.

82. *1st Step.* This chapter should be taught as a direct continuation of the lessons on the degrees of the scale, not as a new subject. For example, taking up the subject at (*c*), § 49, after singing or

playing  and the succession has been named Doh, Ray,

by the class and written in notes, call attention to the fact that the progression has been explained in Chapter II as an interval of a Second. (This forms a Melodic interval; see § 54.) In a similar way, the teacher may proceed up the scale, the next time taking the notes D and E, the third time E and F, etc., being careful that the pupils do not lose sight of the syllabic names. As often as they forget or miss them, return to *Doh*, and let them sing (or recognize) up to the desired notes.

N. B. Being a dissonance, the two notes of the interval of the Second should not be sung together, unless once or twice merely to show their dissonant character.

83. *2nd Step.* Sing or play the notes , requiring the syllabic names as before, and allow them to be written. Explain that this progression forms a Third, and proceed up the scale, taking the notes D and F, E and G, as shown above, requiring first the syllabic names, after which they should be written.

Next, returning to C and E, allow part of the class to sing the lower note, calling it *Doh*, while the remainder sing E, calling it *Me*. This illustrates the *Harmonic* interval, as singing in succession represented the Melodic.

Continue up the scale as before, but now allowing both notes to be sung together and properly written to express the *harmonic* interval.

84. *3rd Step.* Treat Fourths, Fifths, Sixths, Sevenths, and Octaves (not exceeding the limit of the voices) in a similar manner, first Melodically, and then Harmonically.

Carefully call attention to the *musical effect* of the different intervals as well as to the various distances apart.

85. *4th Step.* Sing or play successions of two single notes, requiring first the syllabic names and then the interval.

86. *5th Step.* Play various intervals (harmonic), first striking the notes in succession ("spreading ") if necessary, requiring both the syllabic names and name of the interval. *Let everything be written* as soon as the pupil recognizes it, to gain the habit of expressing his impressions. (Begin this step [§ 86] with Octaves and Fifths.)

87. *6th Step.* Striking a Major Third, change it to Minor by lowering the upper note, calling attention to the different musical effect and the means of producing it; explaining at the same time that some of the Thirds in the scale are Minor without any change, for example, from Ray to Fah, Me to Soh, etc.

88. *7th step.* Display Major and Minor Sixths in a similar manner. Introduce Diminished and Augmented intervals very cautiously, on account of their difficulty.

89. *In general.* Arrange the exercises carefully in point of pro-
gressive difficulty. Do not let the pupil get confused in regard to
the syllabic names. He must have a firm hold of the Tonality. Be
patient.

The pupil may now take two-part songs (or the soprano and alto
of hymns and choruses), and try to think how they would sound,
afterward comparing with the effect when played or sung.

Exercises in Rhythm should be continued.

(Addendum to § 72.)

Complementary Intervals.

Any two intervals which, when added together, form an octave, are
called *Complementary* intervals, since each completes, or complements
the other in the formation of the octave. This is simply another statement of Inversion, for any interval and its inversion form Complementary intervals. *Illustration*:— A Sixth and a Third are Complementary, or the Sixth is said to be Complementary to the Third, and
vice versa. Similarly, Fourths and Fifths, or Seconds and Sevenths,
are Complementary.

PART II.

CHAPTER III.

TRIADS.

The Foundation of the Harmonic System.

NOTE. § 90 is not to be studied. It is designed more especially for the teacher and for those inquiring minds who would know some-thing of the scientific basis of chord-formation, and observe the won-derful symmetry and simplicity of Nature's laws.

Advanced Course.

Harmonics.

90. Science has demonstrated that a musical tone is not one simple sound, but is made up of the combined sounds of many different tones, softly sounding with the principal or Primary tone. It has also been proved that these secondary tones bear a certain relation to the prin-cipal or Primary tone, and though they sound but faintly (being inaudible to untrained ears), can be distinctly recognized by those who are trained in this direction. These secondary or accompanying tones are called *Overtones* or *Harmonics*.

When a long string, tightly drawn, is put into vibration, it vibrates in its full length alone only an instant; after a short time it vibrates also in sections (without interfering with the full-length vibrations) producing higher tones simultaneously with the principal or funda-

mental tone. For illustration, if a string producing the tone

is put into vibration, this tone will be very distinct, but the presence of the following tones, sounding very faintly, can be proved.

Fig. 24.

Primary tone.

---

* These harmonics are not exactly true to pitch.

This series is called the Harmonic Chord, or Nature's Chord Those who are already familiar with chords will observe, that the first six notes sounded together are simply an ordinary chord. If the next note, B♭, is added, a Chord of the 7th is formed. If to the last chord the ninth note of the series is added (the eighth note, C, is merely a duplicate of the lower octaves), a chord of the Ninth is formed. In these three chords, or rather in this one Harmonic Chord, is the *basis of the Harmonic system*, from which the various chord-formations can be logically developed. The above is designed to show four points, viz :—

(*a.*) That a musical tone is made up of many tones sounding together as above stated.*

(*b.*) That a chord, as commonly understood, is an imitation, at the hands of Man, of the great chord of Nature, or at least it has been made to correspond very closely with it.

NOTE. Young students are liable to be troubled by the fact that some of the remoter harmonics are strongly dissonant with the fundamental tone and triad. But this need not disturb them, as the harmonics are more indistinct as they are more remote from the Fundamental tone, and the finest ear cannot detect more than six or seven. Therefore, the upper ones are too weak to have much effect upon a tone, though Science conclusively proves their presence.

(*c.*) That chords are produced by a process of *adding to,* or *building upon, a note called the Fundamental*, or *Root.* The Chord of the 7th was produced by *adding one note to the chord already formed ;* and the Chord of the 9th, by *adding still one more.* -

(*d.*) Conversely, that the chord built upon a Root is considered as *derived from that Root.*

Regular Course.

Triads.

91. When any note is taken, together with the intervals of a Third and a Fifth above it, a Triad is formed. A Triad, then, is a chord of three notes: a Fundamental

---

* There is a strong analogy between a single tone and a ray of light. When thrown through a prism, light is seen to be a compound of various colors, the prism serving to separate the ray into its constituent parts. Similarly, a tone can be shown by the laws of sympathetic vibration to consist of the Primary tone and Overtones, as shown in § 90.

or Root, together with its Third and Fifth, counting up-

ward; e g.,

As shown above, the whole Harmonic System may be said to rest upon this simple Triad. A distinguished musician has declared, "There is but one chord in the world, the Common Triad. All others are merely addi-tions to this."

Exercises.

(*a.*) Write the scale of C, and upon each note, used as a Fundamental, construct a triad, without considering whether the intervals are Major or Minor. (See Fig. 25.)

Fig. 25.

(*b.*) Write similarly the scale of G, F, D, B, etc., not regarding sharps or flats except to place them in the signature, and construct a triad upon each note, as above.

Marking the Triads.

92. In § 2 it was shown how each degree of the scale is numbered from the lowest to the highest. The Triads are described in a similar manner, by indicating upon which degree of the scale they are founded; for exam-ple, "Triad on the 3d degree," " Triad on the 6th degree," etc. For this purpose Roman Numerals are em-ployed, being written under the staff as shown in Fig. 26.

Fig. 26.

I   II   III   IV   V   VI   VII   I

Exercises.

Mark the Triads formed in the exercises in § 91.

Specific Names of Triads.

93. Triads are divided into four kinds, Major, Minor, Diminished, and Augmented. These varieties correspond closely with the intervals of the same names, for they are named, *according to the intervals of which they are composed,* as follows: —

A Major triad has a Major 3rd and Perfect 5th.

A Minor triad has a Minor 3rd and Perfect 5th.

A Diminished triad has a Minor 3rd and Diminished 5th.

An Augmented triad has a Major 3rd and Augmented 5th.

These four kinds of triads are indicated, in marking the triads, as follows:—

Major, by a large Roman numeral, for example: I.

Minor, by a small Roman numeral, for example: ii.

Diminished, by a small Roman numeral with the sign ° affixed: vii°

Augmented, by a large Roman numeral with the sign′ affixed: III′.

Exercises.

(*a.*) Write the Harmonic Minor scale of A, and form triads upon the various steps, as in § 91. Next, describe each triad (Major, Minor, Diminished, or Augmented), and mark as above indicated.

(*b.*) Repeat the process in the Minor scales of E, D, and B.

Principal and Secondary Triads.

94. The triads upon the Tonic, Dominant and Subdominant (see § 34) are called the Principal or Primary Triads, for the following reasons: —

(*a.*) They are most frequently used.

(*b.*) They embrace every note of the scale.

(*c.*) They are sufficient to determine, beyond doubt, the key.

The Triads upon the remaining degrees are called Secondary Triads.

Exercises.

Returning to the exercises in §§ 91, 92, 93, the pupil will describe each Triad, indicating the Secondary Triads by the proper Roman numeral, and the others by the first letter of their names; thus, T, (Tonic); D, (Dominant); and S. D, (Subdominant).

Doubling.

95. In a Triad there are but three different notes. Therefore, if we write music in four parts, one of the three notes must be doubled, i. e., must appear in two parts. *The Fundamental is the best note for doubling, and the Third the poorest.* (See § 162.) The four-part chord resulting from the doubling of one note of the triad is called a Common Chord; e. g.,

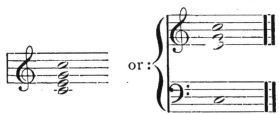

Position.

96. The three notes composing the Triad do not need to be always in the same order, with the Fundamental lowest and the Fifth at the top. The Fundamental or the Third may also occupy the highest place, and the term Position is used to denote which note is highest, as follows :—

(*a.*) When the Fundamental or its octave is highest (in the Soprano) the chord is said to be in the *Position of the Octave.*

(*b.*) When the Third is highest, the Chord is in the *Position of the Third.*

(*c.*) When the Fifth is highest, the chord is in the *Position of the Fifth.*

Fig. 27.

Position of the Octave.   Position of the 3d.   Position of the 5th.

Exercises.

(*a.*) Write the triad upon each of the remaining degrees of the key of C, showing each triad in its three positions, as illustrated in Fig. 27, which gives the triad upon the first degree. Use two staves in writing.

(*b.*) Write Major triads of A, E, F, A♭ and B♭ in the three positions, using the proper (key-) signatures in each case.

Four-part writing ; Connection of Triads.

97. Each chord of four notes is considered as written for a quartet of voices, Bass, Tenor, Alto and Soprano. The Soprano and Bass are called the *Outer* or *Extreme* parts : the Alto and Tenor are called the *Inner* parts. In four-part writing the effect should be considered from two points of view :—

(*a.*) The Melodic effect of each part (as it would sound if sung alone).

(*b.*) The Harmonic effect of the four parts sounding together, and the connection between the successive chords.

Before proceeding to practical exercises in connecting chords and leading the parts, the pupil should learn something of the difficulties in the way of making a good effect, as follows :—

Consecutive Fifths.

98. If we play a series of Thirds, for example,

etc., the effect is not unpleasant. If

we add a Fifth, changing each Third to a triad, thus:

etc., we find the effect harsh and un-

pleasant. This disagreeable effect was evidently not produced by the Thirds sounding in succession, for the

following: etc., is, if possible,

still worse. Therefore, we may conclude that the bad effect is produced by the succession of Fifths.*

Consequently, *Consecutive Fifths are not allowed.*

Consecutive Octaves.

99. Again, if in a four-part chorus two voices sing the same notes, either in unison or an octave apart, there would be in reality but three different parts, which would weaken the harmony. Therefore, *Consecutive Octaves* (*and Unisons*) *are not allowed.*

100. In order to learn how to avoid Consecutive Fifths and Octaves, the pupil should realize that in the progression of the parts, three different movements are possible :—

(*a*.) **Parallel Motion,** in which two parts move in the same direction ; see (*a*), Fig. 28.

(*b*.) **Oblique Motion,** in which one part remains stationary, while the other moves ; see (*b*), Fig. 28.

(*c*.) **Contrary Motion,** in which the parts move in opposite directions : see (*c*), Fig. 28.

---

* The harshness of consecutive 5ths is caused by the suggestion of two different keys in succession without proper (modulatory) connection.

Fig. 28.

In four-part writing, two or even three different kinds of motion can occur simultaneously between the different parts. Parallel motion between three parts is permitted, if no Consecutive Fifths or Octaves result from it. Parallel motion between all four parts is not good, and it is difficult to avoid the forbidden consecutives if the parts all move in the same direction.

To Avoid Consecutive Fifths and Octaves.

Let one or two parts progress in contrary motion to the others.

This rule will cover all cases.

Open and Close Harmony.

101.   When the Soprano, Alto and Tenor all lie within the compass of an octave, the parts are said to be written in *Close* Harmony. If they exceed the compass of an octave, they are in *Open* Harmony

Close Harmony.   Open Harmony.

Fig. 29.

Close Harmony should be used in the following chapters unless otherwise indicated.

To Connect Two Triads.

NOTE. The following is of especial importance, and should be thoroughly mastered before proceeding.

102. Under this head two cases are to be considered:—

(*a.*) *When the two given chords have one or more notes in common.*

(*b.*) *Where there is no common tone* to serve as a connecting-link.

When the Chords have a Note in Common.

Let us take C – E – G and A – C – E, for example, to connect. Having two notes in common, it is evident that there is a close connection between them, and it is only necessary to make this connection apparent to the ear. If we play the two chords thus:

there is to the ear no connection whatever. But when

played thus: the connection is very ap-

parent. This is because the *notes common to both chords are retained in the same parts.* That is, the Tenor and Alto, which have the notes C and E in the first chord, retain them in the second. Therefore, *notes common to both chords are to be retained in the same parts.*

It will be seen, that to follow this all-important principle, the " position " of the chords must be adapted to the necessities of the situation, sometimes one note being highest and sometimes another.

The Process.

103. The following is given to illustrate the mental process by which the beginner should solve every problem. Having written the first chord in notes :—

1st step. What are the notes of the second chord ?*

---

* This question, though unnecessary here, is of importance when the pupil begins to work exercises from a given Bass, as in § 111.

(N. B.   If the pupil has trouble in keeping the notes of the second chord in mind during the following steps, he may write them on a separate slip of paper.)

2nd step.   Is any note common to both chords? What note is it?

3rd step.   In which part (Soprano, Alto, etc.) of the first chord is this " common " note found?   *Ans.* In the— (Here mention whether it is Soprano, Alto Tenor, or Bass), therefore it must appear in the same part in the second chord.

4th step.   Write it, and connect with the same note in the first chord by a tie.   (Do not write any other notes yet.)

5th step.   Name the remaining notes of the second chord.

6th step.   Which "position" of the second chord will enable the remaining notes of the first chord to progress in the smoothest manner to the remaining notes of the second chord ?

Illustration.

104.   To connect the triads C–E–G, written thus: 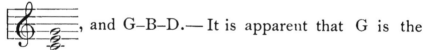, and G–B–D.— It is apparent that G is the " common " note or connecting-link.   Therefore, as G is in the Soprano in the first chord, it must be in the Soprano in the second; according to § 103, 4th step, we have : ___. It is now apparent that the remaining notes of the second chord, B and D, must lie *below* G (as the Soprano is always the highest part), thus : ___. As this makes a smooth leading

of the Alto and Tenor (no wide skips*) the effect is good.

If the first chord is in this position : the connecting note, being G, is in the Alto in the first chord, and must appear in that part in the second chord. Now it is plain that we must *so arrange the remaining notes of the second chord*, B and D, that the Soprano and Tenor of the first chord *will each have a note to which it may progress*; therefore, we cannot place *both* B and D below G, as was the case before, but one should be *above* and one *below*, and the choice of position must depend upon the possibility of making a smooth progression. Let us try with D above and B below, giving : , and compare it with the effect when we place the B above and D below, thus : . It will be seen that although the former will answer, the latter gives the better effect, because there are no skips. Again, taking the first chord in this position : , we find the connecting note in the lowest part; therefore, both the remaining notes of the second chord must be written above the connecting note, giving : .

Exercises.

105. (*a.*) Connect the triad of C with that of F Major,

---

* In the early exercises the parts should not make very wide skips from note to note, but should progress by the smaller intervals (2nds and 3rds) wherever possible. In composition, where the parts progress by the smaller intervals, the effect is restful and tranquil. Where they progress by the larger intervals, such as 4ths, 5th, 6ths, and 8ves, the effect is bolder and more aggressive

taking successively the various positions of the first chord, as illustrated above. Use one staff in writing.

(*b*.) Connect (in three positions) the triad of C maj. with that of E min. ; with A min.

Connect (in three positions) the triad of D min. with that of F maj. ; with A min. ; and with G maj.

Connect (in three positions) the triad of E min. with that of C maj. ; with G maj.

Connect (in three positions) the triad of E min. with that of A min.

Connect (in three positions) the triad of F with triads upon C, A, and D (all in the key of C).

Connect (in three positions) the triad of G with triads upon C, E, and D

Connect (in three positions) the triad of A with triads upon C, D, F, and E.

Connect (in three positions) the triad of B with triads upon E, D, and F.

Note that all the above are in the key of C Major.

(*c*) Transpose (*b*) into other keys, and repeat. (This transposition will not be difficult, if we remember that to transpose a note or a chord it is given the same relative place in the new key that it occupied before being transposed. E. g., if a triad is on the second degree in the key of C, when transposed it must be placed upon the same degree of the new key: if on the fifth degree in the original key, it must be placed upon the same degree in the new key. Likewise the " position " and inversion of a chord must correspond when transposed. If we substitute the Roman Numerals (as shown in § 92) for the letters C, D, E, etc., in exercise (*b*), it will be easy to find the notes corresponding to these numerals in any desired key.

(*d*.) Write (*b*) in four parts, as illustrated in Fig.

30; the root of each chord being written in the Bass, which will remain the same for all positions.

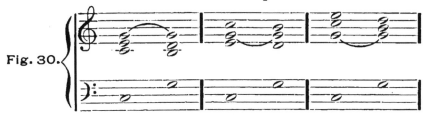

Fig. 30.

To connect two Triads when there is no Common Note.

106. Although two given chords belonging to the same key may not have a visible connection by means of a common note, there is a certain relationship through their being members of the same key, (see the Author's "How to Modulate," § 3,) and with a careful leading of the parts they may be used in succession.

Especial attention must be given to avoid consecutive Fifths and Octaves, remembering that Contrary Motion is the means of so doing. It should be noticed that some Positions are much better than others for a given connection, and that some Positions cannot be used at all. The smoothest connection is usually where the three upper parts move in a direction contrary to the Bass.

The Process.

107. The mental process of finding the correct leading of the parts is somewhat as follows:

Example for illustration. Connect the triad of C, in the position of the 3rd, with the triad of D. Expressed in notes, thus:

(*1st step.*) What are the notes of the Second chord? Ans., D F A.

(*2nd step.*) In which direction does the Bass move in the example? Ans., Upward; therefore it would be well to have the three upper parts (or as many of them as possible) move downward (to move contrary to the Bass).

(*3rd step.*) Which position of the second chord allows the proper progression of the parts, without Consecutive Fifths and Octaves?

(*Or, 3rd step.*) Write the notes of the second chord, so that each part shall progress in the desired direction, avoiding Consecutive Fifths and Octaves.

(*4th step.*) Would any other position give a better leading of the parts, by avoiding large skips or otherwise producing a better general effect?*

N. B. All of the upper parts are not obliged to move contrary to the Bass. Sometimes it is better to have only one part progressing contrary to the Bass.

Fig. 31 illustrates the connection of the triad of C (in its three positions) with that of D.

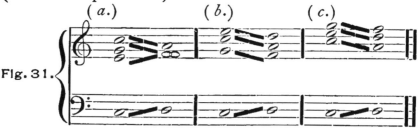

Fig. 31.

(a.)   *(b.)*   *(c.)*

---

* There are other influences affecting the leading of the parts, which are, however, as yet too advanced for the pupil. After having studied as far as §170, the pupil should review this section.

108. At (*a*) it is necessary to double the Third to avoid Consecutive Fifths with the Bass, which would arise if the Alto should progress to A. Notice also that the Tenor should not progress downward to D at this place, as bad hidden Fifths with the Soprano would result. (See § 134.)

Exercises.

109. Copy the following, and fill up the vacant parts, applying the " mental Process " to each of the ten separate examples.

Fig. 32.

Key of C: II   III   III   IV   IV   V   V   VI   VI   VII

N. B.

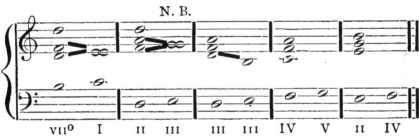

VII⁰   I   II   III   III   III   IV   V   II   IV

At N. B., Fig. 32, the Third was doubled, as the Leading-note should only under exceptional circumstances be doubled (see §162). The above examples do not sound well unless used in connection with other progressions, when they lose much of their harshness. The teacher should give examples in other keys, and as soon as the class can " figure " inversions (see §§ 125 – 132), this section should be again taken up, using chords in their inversions.

Exercises.

(*a*.) In the key of G, connect the triad upon each

degree with the one upon the degree next above, trying the different positions to make the best effect possible.

(*b.*)   Repeat in the keys of B♭, A, and F.

Review of the Connection of Triads.

110.   (*a.*)   Avoid Consecutive Fifths and Octaves.

(*b.*) Contrary motion is the means of avoiding them.

(*c.*)   If there is a connecting note, keep it in the same part in both chords.

(*d.*) If there is no note in common, adopt contrary motion and avoid wide skips, especially guarding against consecutive Fifths and Octaves.

(*e.*)   In doubling notes, the Fundamental is the best note, the Third the poorest.   The Leading-note should be doubled only under exceptional circumstances : though doubling any part is better than open consecutives.

(*f.*)   Avoid wide skips.   Let each part be melodious.

(*g̅.*)   Avoid progressions of Augmented intervals, as they are not melodious.

Part-writing.

111.   Having learned to connect two given triads, the pupil should proceed to put his knowledge into practical use by writing exercises on given Basses.   In these exercises is nothing new ; therefore each exercise may be considered as a little series of examples illustrated in §§ 102 to 110.

N. B.   A figure *over* the *first* Bass note of an exercise, indicates whether the Third, Fifth or Octave of the Bass note is to appear in the Soprano.

Should the pupil need further guidance, the following " mental process, " illustrating Fig. 33, will be of assistance.

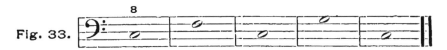

Fig. 33.

112. Process: The Figure 8 over the first note indicates, that we are to begin with the octave (or double octave) of the Root as the highest note, giving the chord in this position:

The first problem then is, to connect this chord with the chord founded on F, as indicated by the second Bass note in Fig. 33. Now let the pupil go through the process shown in §103, giving as a result:

The next problem is to connect the chord last found with the chord founded on C, as indicated by the third note in the given bass. Following the same process brings one more chord. Continuing in the same way gives the completed example:

Fig. 34.

I   IV   I   V   I

113. In the first exercises the Soprano part is given as well as the Bass, leaving the pupil to find the names of the remaining notes in each chord and to place them so that they will progress as smoothly as possible.

The parts should not cross; for example, the Alto should not go higher than the Soprano or lower than the Tenor. Write the exercises in close harmony.

114. The various parts should not exceed the compass of a good voice of corresponding pitch, as shown in Fig 35.

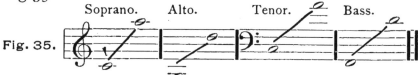

Fig. 35.

The pupil should *always* mark the Roman numerals in the exercises, as shown in Fig. 34. *Always write them before beginning to form the chords*.

115.   Exercises.

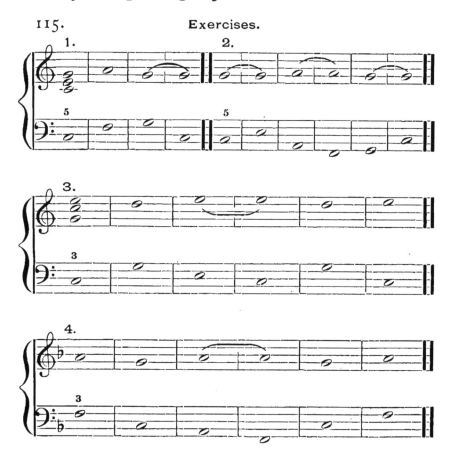

116. In the following exercises the pupil will write the Soprano as well as the other parts. Where the figure 3 is found over the first Bass note in an exercise, it indicates that the first chord should appear in the position of the 3rd. The figure 5 shows that the position of the 5th is desired. Where no figure is given, the position of the octave is to be written. This applies to the first chord only of each exercise.

Exercises.

117. The pupil is recommended to repeat the exercises in this chapter, starting with the Soprano in a different position, in order to realize the different treatment
required by the changed circumstances. It will be found
that some of the exercises cannot be worked out so
smoothly in one position as in another; consequently, by

this practice, the judgment will be sharpened to discern the choice in progressions.

118. In cases where this book is used as a preparation for the study of Analysis, or for Piano-students who are unwilling to study Harmony (part-writing) but who desire to thoroughly understand the construction of the chords, the above exercises may be omitted. In their place the pupil may take Sonatinas, Sonatas, etc., mark the key, indicate upon which degree of the scale each triad is found, and its classification (Major, Minor, etc.). He should be taught, that in considering the harmonic structure of a composition, a broken chord is marked the same as one which is not broken. For example, (*a*), (*b*), and (*c*) of Fig. 36 are all considered to be the chord on C, and are marked accordingly.

Fig. 36.

C: I I . . . . I . . . .

This practice is also recommended to those who take the regular course.

Connection of Triads in Minor Keys.

119. In taking up the Triads of the Minor Scale the principal point for the beginner is to avoid the step of an Augmented Second between the 6th and 7th degrees, where a good connection can be made otherwise. Being a difficult interval to sing, the Augmented Second is not much used in strict writing. For the same reason, all Augmented intervals (in the progression of a single part) are undesirable for the beginner.

Exercises.

(*a.*) Write the harmonic Minor scale of A; place

the Roman Numerals under the notes; form the triads upon each degree as in § 91.

(*b*.) In the following exercises the Roman Numerals will be used to indicate the triads. Instead of saying " Connect the triad on A (or on the 1st degree) with the triad on D (or the 4th degree), we shall say, ·"Connect I with IV," the chord mentioned first being written first and connected with the other one.

(1.)   Connect I with IV; with V; with VI; with II°.

(2.   Connect II° with IV; with VI; with V; with VII°

(3.)   Connect III′ with I; V; VI; VII°.

(4.)   Connect IV with I; II°; V; VI.

(5.)   Connect V with I; III′; VII°.

(6.)   Connect VI with I; II°; III′ : IV.

(7.)   Connect VII° with I; III′; V.

121.   (*c*.) Repeat in the key of C minor: in the key of G minor : in the key of F minor.

122.   In § 41 we learned that the 7th degree of the Minor scale must be raised by an accidental to make a Leading-note to the tonic. This Chromatic Alteration must be indicated in the Bass of the exercises in Minor, and is written as follows :

123.   When a sharp, natural, or flat appears over a given Bass note, it is intended that the note standing a 3rd above that Bass note is to be made sharp, natural, or flat as indicated by the accidental; e. g., Fig. 37, (*a*), (*b*,) (*c*). If the 5th above the Bass note is to be altered, or any other interval, the figure representing the interval to be changed is written with the accidental; e. g., Fig. 37, (*d*), (*e*), (*f*).

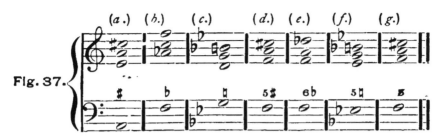

A diagonal line through a figure shows that the interval represented by that figure is to be made sharp; e. g., (*g*), Fig. 37.

Exercises.

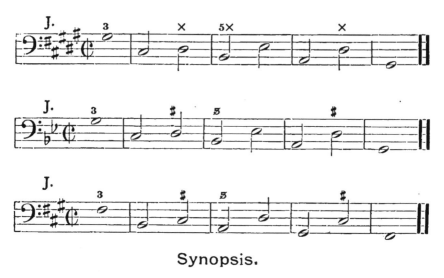

Synopsis.

124.   Form a synopsis of the chapter as usual.

CHAPTER IV.

Inversions of Triads.

125.   It is not necessary that the Fundamental note (or root) of a Triad should always occupy the lowest place.*
The Third or the Fifth can also occupy that place, and when this occurs, the chord is said to be inverted.

When the Fundamental is lowest, the chord is in its Direct form.

When the Third is lowest, the chord is in its 1st Inversion.

When the Fifth is lowest, the chord is in its 2nd Inversion.   (See Fig. 38.)

Notice that " Position " relates to the Soprano or highest part, while " Inversion " relates to the Bass or lowest part.

---

* By inversion the Root is not changed, but transferred to a higher part. The root of a chord is the Bass note only when the chord is not inverted.

Exercises.

(*a.*) Write various Triads, and show their Inversions, as illustrated in Fig. 38. Avoid doubling the Third.

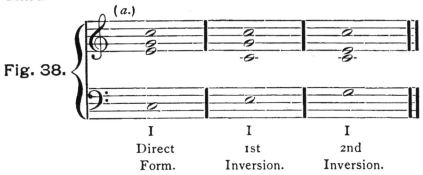

Fig. 38.

| I | I | I |
| Direct Form. | 1st Inversion. | 2nd Inversion. |

126. (*b.*) Write various Triads in their several Inversions and *Positions*, using two staves. The pupil should not forget that Fig. 38 represents not three different chords, *but three forms of one and the same chord.* We could not say (because E is in the Bass) that the form marked " 1st inversion" in Fig. 38 is the triad on E. It is the triad on C in an inverted form. The note C is the fundamental or root from which the chord is derived, which note may be placed lowest or highest. Therefore, in marking the triads, the inversions are to be marked like the direct form (the same Roman numerals), as shown in Fig. 38. The pupil should carefully *distinguish between the actual Bass note, and the root* of the chord. The Bass note changes with each inversion, while the real *root of the chord remains the same for all inversions and positions.*

Figuring Triads.

127. In § 56 the pupil learned to recognize intervals according to their distance from a lower note, and to indicate the same by figures. In a similar manner, whole chords can be figured, by indicating the interval

which each note forms with the Bass or lowest note.
For example, if we have a note with the figures 5 and 3
over it:

we understand that the interval of a Third from the
note C is required, and also the interval of a Fifth, from
the same note. Thus:

If we have the same note with the figures 6 and 4
over it, we should form the intervals of a Fourth and a
Sixth from that note:

128.   These intervals are not necessarily in the same
octave as the Bass note, nor in the exact order indicated by
the figures, as their arrangement depends upon the progression of the parts in preceding chords.

Exercises.

(*a*.)   Figure the chords in Fig. 38.

(*b*.)   Write the scale of C major, and form a triad
upon each degree.   Write each triad in its direct form
and both inversions, using two staves, and writing in
four parts.   Figure each chord thus produced.

(*c*.)   Write on an upper staff (treble) the chords
indicated by the figures over the following Bass notes.

remembering the caution above given in regard to the notes being neither in the same octave as the Bass note, nor in the order expressed by the figures :—

To find the Root of an Inverted Triad.

129. A Triad is formed by taking a note and adding its 3rd and 5th (see § 91) ; and a triad so taken would be figured $\frac{5}{3}$, being in its Direct form. If an inverted triad is taken, the root of which is not known, we can find the root by continuing to invert till the chord can be figured $\frac{5}{3}$, i. e., is in Direct form. When in the Direct form, the root is always the lowest note.

Exercises.

Find the roots of the following chords, and mark each with the proper Roman Numeral :—

130. Notice that the First Inversion of all the triads is figured $\frac{6}{3}$, and the Second Inversion $\frac{6}{4}$. From this fact a chord in its first inversion is often called a " Chord of the Six-Three," or simply a " Chord of the Sixth"; and a chord in its second inversion is called a " Chord of the Six-Four."

Conversely, when a chord is marked $\frac{6}{3}$, we know the Bass note is the Third from the root (in other words, the chord is in its first inversion) ; when marked $\frac{6}{4}$, the Bass is the Fifth from the root, the chord being in the second inversion.

From this (the last preceding statement) the root of the chord may also be found.

Exercises.

Name the roots of the chords expressed by the following :—

131. There are a few conventional rules for Figuring chords, which the pupil must know :—

(*a.*) When no figures are given, the Common Triad is intended.

(*b.*) 6 means the same as $\frac{6}{3}$; a " chord of the Sixth" is the same, therefore, as a " chord of the Six-three."

(*c.*) A sharp, flat, or natural, placed after a figure, is the same as if placed before a note, meaning that the note indicated by the figure is to be made sharp, flat, or natural, as the case may be. If a sharp, flat or natural is given without any figure, the Third from the Bass is intended. A line through a figure, e. g., ♭, is the same as a sharp after it.

(*d.*) The doubling of the parts, positions, leading of the parts, etc., are not indicated by the figuring.

(*e.*) Oftentimes the figures of a chord are not all given, only the characteristic or most important being written, the others being understood, as at (*b*).

(*f.*) In writing a note indicated by a figure, do not consider the key or signature : simply count the degrees of the staff (beginning with the line or space occupied by the Bass note) just as in § 56.

(*g.*) If there are two sets of figures over a given Bass note, it means that the chord represented by the first set of figures is to be followed by the chord represented by the second set while the Bass is held, the time-value of the Bass note being divided between the two chords; e. g.,

Exercises.

132. Applying the above rules, fill out four-part chords from the following figured Basses, also marking each chord with the proper Roman Numeral. (There is no connection between the successive chords.)

Exercises in Part-writing, introducing Inversions and Figured Bass.

133. The mental processes described in §§ 103 and 107, should be carefully applied in the following exercises. One question might be added to the process when considering inversions, viz. : "What is the root of the chord, and upon which degree of the scale is it (the root) ?" In every case the chord should be marked with the proper Roman Numeral (which must appear as the answer to the above questions) before proceeding with the connection of chords.

N. B. When a chord appears successively in two different positions or inversions, it is obvious that the rule in § 102 (to keep the common notes in the same parts) cannot be obeyed, e. g.,

This rule is also occasionally broken in connecting two *different* chords, to secure a good progression of the parts. In general, it will be found that the different rules must yield one to another as circumstances demand. (See §§ 161 et seq.)

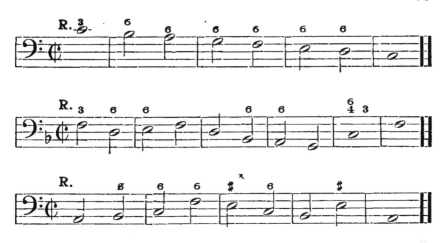

Hidden Octaves and Fifths.

134. Hidden Octaves and Fifths occur when two parts, moving in parallel motion, strike an octave or fifth. If the notes over which they pass should be written out, consecutives would appear. Although not so disagreeable as open consecutives, and not positively forbidden, Hidden Consecutives are better avoided, unless by their use a better progression can be obtained.

The effect of Hidden Octaves or Fifths between the two outer parts is much worse than between the inner parts, or between one inner and one outer part.

Where both parts skip to the Octave or Fifth, the effect is worse than if one moves diatonically to its place. Hidden Octaves and Fifths arising as shown in Fig. 39 are freely permitted.

Hidden Octaves.   Hidden Fifths.

Fig. 39.

The pupil should not attempt to avoid hidden 5ths and 8ves altogether, but should discriminate in regard to the effect, rejecting those that are harsh. Contrary motion will usually be of assistance in avoiding them, but the pupil should know that an awkward progression of a part is worse than the hidden consecutives, and choose the lesser of two evils.

Exercises.

Harmonizing the Scales.

135. An excellent exercise, at every stage of advancement, is the practice of harmonizing the scales in every

key, and using as many different chords and as much variety as the pupil may have studied at the time. It will be noticed that every note of the scale may belong to three different chords, and either one of these three chords may be used to harmonize that note if a smooth connection with the preceding and following chords can be made.

The scale to be harmonized should be written sometimes in the Bass and sometimes in the Soprano, (see examples below). [For advanced pupils it may also be written in the Alto and Tenor.] When written in the Bass, it should be observed that there can be no common notes to connect two successive chords. unless chords of the 7th are used, for which see later chapters.

Exercises.

(*a.*) Fill out the four parts in the following :—

(*b.*) Harmonize the ascending scale of C in as many ways as possible, using only the triads with their inversions.

(*c.*) Harmonize the descending scale in a similar manner.

(*d.*) Harmonize similarly the ascending and descending scales in all other keys.

· (*e.*) *Advanced Course.* Harmonize similarly the Minor scales.

Synopsis.

136. Write a synopsis of the chapter as at the end of Chapter III.

The Perceptive Faculties.

Continued from page 40.

Triads.

137. After teaching the pupils to recognize two tones sounding together, it is but a step further to recognize three tones. This section is merely a continuation of the foregoing, and may be treated somewhat as follows :—

1st *Step.* (*a.*) Teacher sounds the note C, and says : "This tone is Doh. Write it in the key of — —" (mentioning any key, not necessarily the key of C).

(*b.*) Teacher sounds E and asks, " What is this tone ?"— *Ans.* *Me.* —" Write it."— Two pupils sing Doh and Me.

(·*c.*) Teacher sounds G and asks, "What is this tone ?"— *Ans.* *Soh.* " Write it."— Third pupil sings Soh. Three pupils sing the three notes together.

(*d.*) While the chord is being sounded, the teacher says, " Remainder of the class sing Me ; (sing Soh ; sing Doh). Which note is highest ? — Which is lowest ? — Which between ?"

In this way the pupils learn to hear and distinguish the individual notes from the mass of sound, for as soon as they have sung them a few times while the chord is sounding, they will be able to hear the individual tones, and thus recognize the component parts of a chord.

The teacher should not confine himself to the triad on C, but may take any Major triad in the middle of the keyboard or of the voices. The note which is represented by Doh should always be announced, to give a starting-point.

138. *2nd Step.* Having trained the pupils to recognize the notes of the triad by the above and other exercises which his ingenuity or the necessities of the case may suggest, the teacher should proceed to train the pupils to recognize the *different positions of the Triad.*

Process :— (*a.*) Teacher sounds triad C – E – G, and asks, "What are the syllabic names of these tones ?— Which is highest ? — Which lowest ?"

(*b.*) Teacher sounds same triad, but in position of the Octave, repeating the change to make it forcible, as follows :

and asks, " Which note is highest in the last chord ? — Which is lowest ?—Which between ?" Require the pupils to sing the notes one by one, using the syllabic names, while the chord is sounding. Also ask them to fix their attention strongly on one individual note in the chord, while the teacher plays the chord, and try to hear it, i. e., to individualize the note from the chord, and thus cultivate the perceptions.

In the same manner the remaining positions should be taught.

139. *3rd Step. Chords of four tones.*

(*a.*) Let three pupils sing the triad C – E – G. Teacher sounds C (3rd space, treble) and asks, " What is this note ?"— *Ans.* Doh.— " Which Doh ?"— *Ans.* Octave above the first Doh.— Fourth pupil sings upper Doh. Four pupils sing, forming the chord, while remainder of class sing single tones as before. Teacher asks, " Which note is highest ? — Which is lowest ?— Which is intermediate ? Which note is doubled ?"

NOTE. The piano may be used to produce the chord, but it is far preferable to have it sung.

Proceed as above with other two positions.

140. *4th Step.   Inversions.*

Play the following, asking questions as before, concerning the highest and lowest notes, etc.:

Then play the passage next given, calling attention to the movement of the bass, and to the different musical effects of the different inversions, wrong doubling at ×, etc.   Repeat with other Major chords, asking questions as above.

141. *5th Step.   Minor Triads.*
         Play ·

calling attention to the different effect of the Minor, showing how it differs from the Major, asking questions as above, etc.   Take in succession the Minor triads of the key of C (also other keys), and question in regard to highest and lowest notes, etc.

142. *6th Step.   Progression of a part.*

Play little progressions where a single part moves, requiring the class to recognize which part moves and what the progression is. (The answers should be in syllabic names, and the notes written as recognized.)   To illustrate, play :

Process : — First name the notes in the first chord ; ascertain the position and inversion, and write the notes. Then study the progression.

Next take up examples where two parts move without change of chord ; e. g.,

Lack of space prohibits the multiplication of these simple examples, which can be taken from many sources or invented by the teacher. Many examples should be studied before proceeding.

143. *7th Step. Progression of parts with change of chords.*

(*a.*) *Without Inversions.* Give some examples, if necessary selecting from the first exercises in part-writing (§ 113, etc.), calling especial attention to the progression of the Bass ; for if that can be ascertained, the fundamental of each chord is clear, and with it the chord itself, though the position may remain in doubt. (The position will be discovered by requiring the pupils to sing the notes of the chord, using the syllabic names.)

Notice also the progression of the Soprano, whether up or down.

The first exercises should consist of but two chords — one progression, — and should illustrate the progression from the Tonic to the Dominant or Sub-dominant, after which the progression from the Tonic to the remaining degrees of the scale may be studied, and later exercises may be extended to take in several progressions. It is of especial importance that the exercises be carefully written.

144. (*b.*) *Progressions with Inversions.*

This is more difficult than the preceding, and requires patience on the part of both teacher and pupil. At first give chords, the natural progression of which can be easily traced, as for example those given here. Those progressions are best which have some tied notes,

as the attention can be concentrated on one or two moving parts. Simple, well-known harmonies only should be used, leaving the more difficult ones till a later period. The teacher should constantly lead and direct the perceptions by questions as illustrated above. Each step should be expressed in notes.

145. It will be advantageous at this point for the pupil to refer to the exercises he has already written, and try to think, from looking at the progressions, how they would sound. Indeed, he should never look at a chord without trying to realize its effect.

NOTE. The treatment of the Perceptive faculties is here given, not as a complete exposition of the subject, but merely as a suggestive outline, to be expanded and adapted by the teacher to the needs of individual cases.

Transposition.

146. The pupil will gain a practical idea of Transposition through the exercises used in developing the perceptive faculties, if the teacher will vary the keys in which the pupil writes what he hears. For example, the teacher may say when beginning an exercise, " This tone is Doh " (striking some note) ; " write in the key of G." After a few moments he may say, *without changing the pitch of Doh*, " Write in the key of *F*", and the pupils will soon find that they can as well express the relations of the notes to each other in one key as in another.

IMPORTANT NOTE.

In this book the chords of the Dominant 7th, Diminished 7th, Major and Minor 9th, and the Augmented $\frac{6}{3}$, $\frac{6}{4}$, and $\frac{6}{5}$, are treated as *different forms of the same chord*, having the same root, same dissonant intervals, and same resolution. In learning the natural resolution of dissonant intervals in general, the proper resolution of all these chords is learned, thus simplifying and systematizing the subject to a remarkable degree. Therefore, study Chapter V thoroughly, repeating again and again, if necessary, till the subject is really clear.

———

CHAPTER V.

CHORDS OF FOUR NOTES : THE CHORD OF THE SEVENTH.

Its Construction.

147. As stated in § 90, the whole system of chords is a process of building, or adding upper notes to some note considered as a Root (Foundation, or Fundamental). The various triads were formed by adding a 3rd and a 5th to such a Root-note. If we add not only the 3rd and the 5th, but also the interval of a 7th to the Root-note or Fundamental, we shall have a *Chord of the Seventh*.

To illustrate, represents the root G with its 3rd and 5th forming a triad. If the interval of a 7th (from G) is also added, we have , called a Chord of the Seventh. (It may be noticed in reference to this building-process, that each note is at the interval of a 3rd — either Major or Minor — from the note next below. In the following chapters it will be seen that this same rule of placing the successive notes a 3rd apart is followed in forming chords of the Ninth; also in what are called, by some theorists, the chords of the Eleventh and the Thirteenth.)

As the character of Triads differs according to the character of the component intervals, (Major, Minor, etc., see § 93,) so the character of the Chords of the Seventh must differ, since they are nothing more than triads with the addition of one more interval.

Exercises.

148.   (*a.*)   Write chords of the 7th upon every note of the Major scales of C, G, F, and D, describing the character of the triad as in § 93, and indicating, on a separate line, the character of the 7th.   For example, forming the chord of the 7th on the third degree of the scale of C, it would be described as in Fig. 40.

Fig. 40.

III with
Minor Seventh.

The Roman Numeral, being small, indicates that the triad is Minor.   The character of the 7th is plainly expressed.

(*b.*)   Write chords of the 7th upon every note of the Minor scales of A, E, D, and B, indicating the character of the triad and the 7th as above.

149.   The pupil, while writing the above, should notice the following :—

(1.)   That some of the chords, particularly in the Minor keys, sound so badly that they could not be used.

(2.)   That the chord of the 7th formed upon the 5th degree, the Dominant, *is alike in Major and Minor,* and is not only the most agreeable one, but is the only one having a Major 3rd and Minor 7th.

(3.) That none of the chords of the 7th are satisfactory to rest upon, but, like the Augmented and Diminished intervals and triads, seem to require something to come after them to create a feeling of repose.

Fig. 41.

For example, the chord (*a*), in Fig. 41, although it sounds well, is evidently not satisfactory to dwell upon, or to use as the final chord of a composition, as it seems to suggest something which should follow to make it complete. Notice that the chord marked (*b*) gives this sense of completeness and repose.

150. This leads us to consider that all chords may be divided, with respect to this quality (repose or the lack of it), into two kinds : *Independent chords*, or those which are satisfactory to pause upon ; and *Dependent chords*, or those which demand that some chord should follow to establish repose. This classification corresponds with the division of intervals into Consonant and Dissonant (see § 75), for those chords containing *consonant intervals exclusively* are *Independent*, while those containing *even one dissonant interval* are *Dependent* chords.

151. This demand on the part of a Dependent chord to be followed by something reposeful, is satisfied if a consonant chord succeeds it. The process of passing

from a Dependent chord to one that is consonant (Inde‑
pendent) is called "*resolving*" it, and the chord to
which it progresses is called the "*chord of resolution.*"

It is necessary to resolve dissonances, not only
because they are unsatisfactory to rest upon, but also be‑
cause there are *tendencies on the part of certain inter‑
vals contained in them, and of certain notes of the
scale, to progress in definite directions.**

The Principle of Tendencies: Melodic Tendencies.

152. (*a.*) This tendency of certain notes of the scale
to progress in definite directions may be illustrated by sing‑
ing the Major scale up to and including the 7th degree, then
suddenly pausing without singing the remaining (8th)
degree. By thus pausing, a sense of incompleteness will
be felt,— a desire for the delayed note. Thus it is clear
that the 7th degree has a strong tendency to progress to
the 8th degree, which is the Tonic, or *most perfect
resting-place in the whole scale.* On account of this
marked tendency toward the tonic (or its octave), the 7th
degree of the scale is called the *Leading-note.*

(*b.*) Similar experiments will show that the 3rd
degree of the scale has a distinct tendency to ascend,
though the tendency is not so strong as in the case of the
7th degree; and that the 4th degree tends downward.

(*c.*) An accidental sharp tends to continue upward,
and an accidental flat downward. (N. B. When a nat‑
ural is used to raise a note already flatted by signature
or otherwise, it is like a sharp in its effect, and has the
same tendency to ascend. Likewise, when a natural is

---

* In fact, the reason that some chords are unsatisfactory to pause upon is
simply because certain intervals and notes have the above-mentioned tenden‑
cies; for while perfectly agreeable to listen to, they point unmistakably toward
something which is to follow.

used to depress a note already sharped, it is like a flat in its effect, and has the same tendency to descend.) Notes having a tendency to progress in a particular direction, are called *Tendency-notes.*

Tendency of Continuity.

153. A tendency to progress in any desired direction may be given to a note, or a natural tendency counteracted, *by approaching that note from a contrary direction.* Thus, if it is desired to have the 7th degree progress downward, it can be done by approaching it from above:

 . This might be called the *Tendency of Continuity*, i. e., to continue in a given direction after having started.

Harmonic Tendencies.

154. An *Harmonic Tendency* is the tendency of a dissonant interval, or of the notes forming it, to progress in certain definite directions.   It is apparent that the natural (Melodic) tendencies of the above named Tendency-notes are not so strong but that they may be overcome by the tendency of Continuity.   But, when this natural tendency is *heightened by the presence of dissonant intervals,* the demand for progression is quite unmistakable. Let us examine the effect of dissonant intervals upon the tendency to progress.

(1)   Play the following and pause:

the ear will then demand that G♯ shall progress to A This is caused, first, by the fact that in touching G♯ we have started on the road from G to A, and having completed half the distance (theoretically a little more than half), it is only natural to desire to continue to the destination. It would be useless to go half-way, and then turn back. (See § 152, *c.*) Secondly, it is caused by the fact that we have at x a perfect 5th, followed by an augmented 5th. The perfect 5th has been made larger by a sharp, and it would be expected to develop into something else instead of retreating. Thus it is apparent that the *combined* influences at work must create a demand for a chord to follow any dependent chord.

(2.) Again, striking the interval at (*a*), Fig. 42, we find a strong tendency to progress to the interval at (*b.*) This is caused by the same *tendency of an augmented interval* (here an augmented 4th) *toward a further digression of the parts.*

Fig. 42.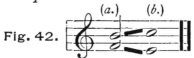

(3.) On the other hand, if we take a Normal interval and diminish it, there is a strong tendency to *still further contract*, as in Fig. 43, where (*a*) is the Normal interval, (*b*) the diminished and (*c*) the result of the tendency toward further contraction.

Fig. 43.

These are illustrations of *Harmonic Tendencies.*

To formulate the illustrations in Figs. 42 and 43, the following is given :—

All Augmented intervals tend toward further expansion.

All Diminished intervals tend toward further contraction.

Note. This law is a direct result of the principles stated in §§ 152 (*c*) and 153.

Advanced Course.

From the above it will be seen that there is an e..ceedingly close connection between Melodic and Harmonic Tendencies. In fact, an Harmonic Tendency might be defined as the resu't or effect produced by the presence of a Melodic Tendency-note in a *dissonant* interval. The dissonance serves to heighten and emphasize the tendencies of the single tones.*

Regular Course.

155. In § 75 it was stated, that Dissonant intervals were so named on account of their unrestful effect, requiring or pointing to some other interval to follow. It may also be stated, that *the natural tendency of a dissonant interval is to progress to the* nearest *consonant interval belonging to the key*, the tones moving according to the principles shown in §§ 152 – 154.

As chords are made up of intervals, it follows, that dissonant (i. e., Dependent) chords are those which contain dissonant intervals, and the natural resolution of a chord depends upon the tendencies of the dissonant intervals contained in it.

Now, let us apply our knowledge of Tendencies to the Chord of the Dominant Seventh.

Chord of the Dominant Seventh: Resolution of Dissonances: Application of the Principles of Tendencies: Cadencing Resolution.

156. The chord of the 7th which is founded on the 5th degree of the Major and Minor scales, has already been mentioned as being the most agreeable of all chords of the Seventh, and is peculiar in being the only one having a Major 3rd and a Minor 7th. Having a very close relationship with the chord on the Tonic (see §§ 158

---

* A consonant interval, being restful in its nature (see § 75), would serve to *hide* rather than to emphasize the melodic tendencies of the single tones.

and 266), this chord plays an important part in forming a key, and is called the chord of the Dominant ("ruling") Seventh. The pupil is, of course, already familiar with this chord, as it is used very frequently.

157.   According to the principles stated in § 155, it becomes necessary to examine the structure of the chord of the Dominant 7th, and find its dissonant intervals, if we would understand its resolution. Taking the chord in the order in which it is constructed, let us examine it in detail. From G to B is a Major 3rd, which is a consonance; from G to D is a Perfect 5th, which is also a consonance; from G to F is a Minor 7th, and here we find the first dissonant element, for we have learned that sevenths are dissonances (see § 75). Again, starting from the second note of the chord, B, we find that from B to D is a Minor 3rd, a consonance: from B to F is a diminished 5th, forming a dissonance. Here, then, is the second dissonant element. Further, starting from the third note of the chord, from D to F is a Minor 3rd, a consonance.

We have learned that the character of a chord (consonant or dissonant) depends upon the character of the intervals contained in it. Therefore, we see that the reason this chord is dissonant is, that it contains the dissonant intervals of a Minor 7th from G to F, and of a Diminished 5th from B to F.   (Notice that if the note F were absent, there would be no dissonant intervals; i. e., the addition of a 7th to the triad changes an *Independent* Triad to a *Dependent* Seventh-Chord.)

The tendencies of these dissonant intervals, in regard to resolution, are as follows:—The tones of the Diminished 5th: tend to approach (§ 154), F progressing downward to the next step, and B upward

. The minor 7th: tends also

to converge, F passing downward, while G remains

stationary, or may progress upward;
.

In addition to these Harmonic tendencies, we must also consider the Melodic tendencies mentioned in § 152. Here we have the Leading-note, B, tending strongly upward, and the fourth degree of the scale, F, tending slightly downward. As these Melodic tendencies agree perfectly with the Harmonic tendencies, the natural resolution of the chord becomes clear. Let it be noticed, that the tones without any special tendency may progress either upward or downward, or may remain, as may be necessary either to avoid consecutive 5ths or 8ves, *or to fill up the chord of resolution to advantage.* In accordance with the natural resolution of the dissonant intervals, the resolution of the chord is as follows:—

V7   I

In the different positions of the chord, although the notes may change their mutual intervallic relationship (e. g., by inverting the intervals), the tendencies and progressions of the individual tones remain quite the same as above described. Fig. 44 shows the different positions of the chord of the Dominant 7th, with their natural resolutions.   Notice that in every position the Leading-note, B, progresses upward, while F, the 4th degree of the scale, moves downward.   Notice, also, that the interval of a Diminished 5th, B — F, at (*a*) and (*b*), Fig. 44, appears inverted, i. e., an Augmented 4th, F — B, at (*c*) and (*d*), the augmented interval expanding for its resolution, and the Diminished contracting ; *while the progression of the individual tones remains the same* (i. e., B moves to C, and F to E, in both cases).

Fig. 44.
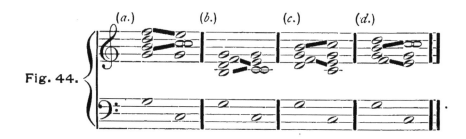

N. B.   The *natural* resolution of these intervals is *always the same;* therefore, wherever we find them, whether in chords of the Dominant 7th, Diminished 7th, Minor 9th, or Augmented 6th, we may expect them to *resolve just the same.*   When they do not follow this natural resolution, there is a reason for it, explained in §§ 161 to 169, and 192 to 198 ; but the *principle remains unchanged.*

The Natural or Cadencing Resolution.

158.   In § 156 we noticed the close relationship of the Chord of the Dominant Seventh to the Tonic triad.   It will now be observed, that the tendencies of the tones F and B in Fig. 44 are toward E and C respectively, *which are parts of the tonic triad,* while G may remain, thus completing the triad.   When the chord of

the Dominant seventh is resolved thus to the Tonic Triad, the resolution is called the Cadencing Resolution.*

If the above-mentioned tendencies are respected, and the remaining parts are led as smoothly as possible,** avoiding unnecessary skips and consecutive 5ths and 8ves, the pupil will not need detailed rules, other than those already given, for the following exercises. One or two hints may, however, be of service.

Remember that it is better to double the Fundamental or 5th of a chord than the 3rd. Sometimes the 5th of the final chord must be omitted to secure a good leading of the parts, another note being doubled in its stead; or the 5th of the chord of the Dominant Seventh may not appear, for the same reason. (This also applies occasionally to the triads.)

Exercises.

(*à.*) Fill out the chords marked I in Fig. 45, leading the parts upward or downward as indicated by the diagonal lines;*** and explain the tendencies as above.

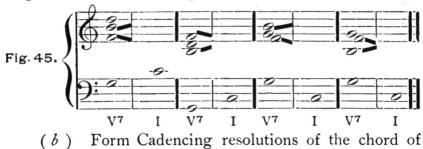

Fig. 45.

V⁷   I   V⁷   I   V⁷   I   V⁷   I

(*b*) Form Cadencing resolutions of the chord of

---

* It should be observed, that the triad on C is the resolution of the Chord of the Seventh upon G, and that C is a 4th higher than G. Therefore, when *any* Chord of the Seventh resolves to the Triad a 4th higher (or a 5th lower), this is said to be a Natural or Cadencing resolution. (See § 190.)

** The pupil should carefully note the difference between progression and resolution. A resolution is a progression, but is influenced by the presence of dissonant intervals, and is therefore not free. A resolution implies the presence of a dissonance in the previous chord.

*** In the natural resolution, the dissonant tones (and, in fact, all the tones) must move *diatonically*. (See § 3, foot-note, and § 44).

the Dominant Seventh in four positions, in the key of F; in the key of G; of B♭; of A; of D; of F♯. Designate the tendency-notes by heavy lines indicating the direction in which they resolve, as shown in Fig. 45.

159.   In the first foot-note of § 158, it is shown that a chord of the Dominant 7th resolves to the triad a 4th higher.   Conversely, if we would find that Chord of the Dominant 7th which shall resolve to any desired triad, we need merely to look for the note a 4th lower than the Root of the triad to find the Root of that chord of the 7th which shall resolve to the triad in question ; and, having the root we can build the chord as shown in § 147.

Exercises.

Name the Root of the chord of the Dominant 7th which shall resolve to the triad of D; write the whole Chord of the 7th and resolve it.

Name the Root and write the Chord of the 7th which shall resolve to the triad of A; of G; of B♭; of F♯; of A♯; of B; of F; etc.

Exercises.

160.   In the following exercises the Chord of the 7th will be indicated by the figure 7 over the bass.

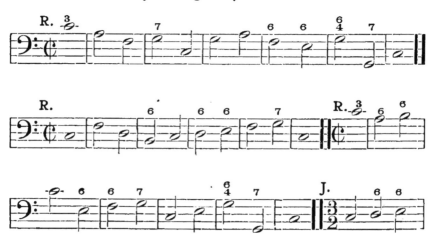

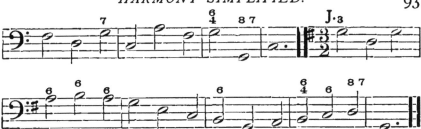

The Principles of Part-leading: "Influences," Combined and Opposed.

161. It has been said that the rules of Harmony were made only to be broken, and that every rule has more exceptions than applications. It would seem better, therefore, to review the principles from which the rules are derived, and thus gain a sound judgment in regard to the leading of the parts, which must ultimately replace any rules that could be given.

The sources of the rules which are commonly given, are found in the *necessity of considering the following points in order to produce good effect in part-writing·*

(1.) The Harmonic effect of the four parts together.

(2.) The Melodic effect of the individual parts.

} (See §97.)

(3.) The Tendencies of certain notes of the scale, and of various dissonant intervals; i. e., the Melodic and Harmonic Tendencies. (See §§ 152 to 155.)

(4.) The bad effect of Consecutive 5ths and 8ves.

(5.) The bad effect of doubled 3rds.*

(6.) The Prominence of Outside Parts.**

(7.) The desirability of Connection between successive chords.

(8.) The arrangement of the notes in a chord; i. e., their distance apart.***

---

*: **: ***: See the following paragraphs.

The above-mentioned points may be called, for convenience, " Influences " which affect or control the leading of the parts. Sometimes these various Influences
agree, or combine to demand the same progression; sometimes they oppose one another.

Notes upon the Preceding.

162. *By doubling the 3rd a certain dissonant overtone (See § 90;
and Note, p. 44) is brought into prominence, making the chord somewhat rough in effect. Therefore it is not well to double the 3rd without some definite reason.

Furthermore, in the Tonic triad, and also in the Dominant triad
or Chord of the 7th, chords which appear very frequently, the 3rd is a
tendency-note. (See § 152.) Now, it will be seen that tendency-notes
should never be doubled, if possible to avoid it, as the result must be
either consecutive 8ves or the contradiction of the tendency by one of
the notes. Therefore, where the 3rd is a tendency-note, it should not
be doubled. Where it is not a tendency-note, it may be freely doubled
if thereby a better leading of the parts is obtained. (The chief Tendency-notes (Melodic) of a scale are the 3rd and 7th. When the 3rd
of a chord happens to be one of these notes, it is better not doubled.)

163. **It will be observed, that the Soprano and Bass parts are
more conspicuous than the inner parts. Therefore, that which might
be allowed in the inner parts may be found very disagreeable — and
consequently be forbidden, — when occurring in the outer parts. Included in the above are found most frequently the two points of
(*a.*) Disregarded tendencies : e. g.,

Fig. 46.

At (*a*), Fig. 46, the upward tendency of the Leading-note, B, is
disregarded, it being led down to G, with very bad effect. At (*b*) the
same thing is done, but in an inner part. The effect here is very good,
as the Alto, an inner part, is less prominent than the Soprano, and as
the note to which the Leading-note would have progressed is still

found in the last chord. Again, by the progression of the Alto Leading-note down to G, the last chord has the 5th which would otherwise be lacking.

(*b.*) Hidden Consecutives: e. g.,

Fig. 47.

The progression at (*a*), Fig. 47, is too harsh to be effective, the hidden consecutives appearing in the outer parts; but the progression at (*b*) is much more agreeable, as the hidden consecutives are between one inner and one outer part. Also, where the natural tendency of a note is disregarded, the effect of a Hidden Consecutive is less likely to be agreeable than where the tendency has not been disturbed. When considering the introduction of a Hidden Consecutive, this point should be considered. In the example, the downward tendency of F (the 4th degree of the scale) is disregarded, with bad effect where the neglect is made prominent by being in the Soprano. In the Alto it is less disagreeable, though it is easily seen that the effect of such progressions might be made still better by observance of the Tendencies

Distribution of the Parts.

164. ***To produce the best effect, the notes of a chord should be at about an equal distance from each other. If necessary to distribute them unequally, the larger intervals should be in the lower parts. Excepting between the Bass and Tenor, there should not be more than an octave between two neighboring parts. Play the following :

Bad.   Good.

Opposition of Influences.

165. An illustration of this opposition is given in Fig. 48. In this example there is a tendency on the part of the Leading-note, B, to ascend. If this tendency is followed, the next chord will have no 5th.

Fig. 48.

As in some cases (for example in a full chorus) this would weaken the effect of the four voices singing together — see " Influences 1 and 8 " — it is sometimes better to sacrifice the upward tendency of the Leading-note in order to gain a full effect in the following chord, giving the progression :

In disregarding an Influence as was just shown, the pupil should guard against violating some other Influence ; for example, if the Leading-note were in the Soprano or Bass, it could not progress downward on account of Influence 6. The effect would be very bad, as shown in Fig. 46, (*a*).

Again, if the Bass note G, in Fig. 48, should progress *downward* to C, instead of upward, the leading-note could not pass downward, on account of the bad Hidden 5ths (both parts moving by a skip, see § 134); e. g.,

166. Another illustration of the manner in which these influences may oppose each other is shown in Fig. 49.

Fig. 49.

At x the 3rd of the chord, E, is doubled, in opposition to Influence 5. The reason for this is shown in Influence 2, namely, the advantage of a smooth progression of the parts : also in Influence 4, for if the Tenor note, E, in the chord marked x, be changed to C in order to avoid doubling the 3rd, the result would be Consecutive 5ths with the Alto, which are much worse than a doubled 3rd. Contrary motion and the *Tendency of Continuity* combine to prevent any bad effect which might be expected from doubling this Tendency-note.*

167. One more illustration may be given : — Influence 7 recommends the retention of a common note in the same part (see also § 102). But it occasionally happens, that other considerations, particularly Influences 2 and 8, are more important, and demand that this Influence be sacrificed for them. This is shown in Fig. 50. Here the note C, which in the first chord is taken by the Tenor, is in the second·chord taken by the Alto.**

Fig. 50.

---

* A Melodic Tendency may be disregarded far more freely than an harmonic tendency, since the former can be removed by Continuity. (See § 153.)

** If circumstances should allow the rearrangement of the first chord, it would still be possible to retain the common note ; e. g.,

This would illustrate the fact that in writing exercises, if the pupil finds it difficult to make a certain connection, by going back a few chords and working in a different position, a way may be opened.

Many other illustrations might be given, showing how circumstances alter cases, and that what is good in one place may not be
best in another. The pupil should understand that part-writing is not
a question of following rules, but is a matter of judgment, controlled
by the considerations above mentioned.

In general the pupil will find that the more prominent of the
above Influences are Nos. 3, 4, 6, and 7.

General Directions for Part-writing.

168.   In summing up the above, and formulating directions for Part-leading which shall be simple and yet
adapted to all cases, the following may be given:—

(1)   Avoid Consecutive 5ths* and 8ves.

(2.)   Avoid Hidden 5ths and 8ves only when they
make a bad effect.

(3.)   A note common to two chords is to be retained
in the same part, unless some other Influence requires
another progression.

(4.)   Smooth progressions are better than wide
skips in the parts.

(5.)   Study the Influences. If they agree, there
will be no question in regard to the progression. If they
disagree, let the stronger rule unless consecutives are produced.

(6.)   Listen to the effect. If it is bad probably some
Influence has been disregarded.

169.   From this time forward, the teacher, when cor-
recting exercises, should designate which Influence has

---

* A single exception may be given. A Perfect 5th may be followed by a
Diminished 5th, thus, , but not reversed, thus,

Good.

Bad.

been disregarded in each case; or he may simply draw a line through the wrong note and mark the number of the Influence which, if followed, will rectify the error, leaving the pupil to change it. This will awaken the critical powers, and cultivate the judgment. Also allow the pupils to correct one another's work according to the same plan, in each case giving the reason for the correction.

NOTE. The pupil should distinguish carefully between the chord of the Dominant seventh *on* G and the chord of the Dominant seventh *in the key* of G. The former has the note G for its root; while the latter is built upon the 5th degree (the dominant) of the scale of G, i. e., D.

Exercises.

170. Mark the Roman Numerals under the Basses before proceeding.

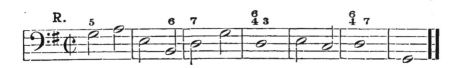

Exercises in Harmonizing the Scale.

171.   Harmonize the Major and Minor scales, using
the chords of the 7th where possible, and the triads with
their inversions.

Synopsis.

Write the usual Synopsis of the chapter.

CHAPTER VI.

INVERSIONS OF THE CHORD OF THE SEVENTH.

172. We have repeatedly seen the different Positions of the Chord of the Seventh. We will now consider the Inversions, which are very similar to the Inversions of Triads, though a little more complicated, owing to the presence of four notes in the chord. Compare the following with § 125.

(*a.*) When the Root is in the Bass, the chord is in its *Direct form*.

(*b.*) When the Third is in the Bass, the chord is in its 1*st Inversion*.

(*c.*) When the Fifth is in the Bass, the chord is in its 2*d Inversion*.

(*d.*) When the Seventh is in the Bass, the chord is in its 3*rd Inversion*.

The Inversions are figured and named as follows:—

Direct.	1st Inversion.	2nd Inversion.	3rd Inversion.
7	6 6	6 4	6
5 or 7	5 or 5	4 or 3	4 or 2
3	3	3	2
	Six-Five-Three,	Six-Four-Three,	Six-Four-Two,
	or	or	or
	Six-Five.	Four-Three.	Second.

Example :

	7	6 6	6 4	6
		5 or 5	4 or 3	4 or 2
		3	3	2

Exercises.

(*a.*)   Write the Chord of the Seventh upon each degree of the key of G, in its several inversions, and figure them.   (The positions should vary in the different exercises.)

(*b*)   Write the same in the keys of D and F.

To find the Root of a Given Chord of the Seventh.

Proceed as shown in § 129.   When the chord is in its " Direct form," it is said to be placed in 3rds, since each note is a 3rd above the one next below.   It should be noticed that when placed in its Direct form, a chord is always figured $\frac{7}{3}$, or such part of these figures as may be necessary.   If either of the figures 2, 4, or 6 appears, an *inversion,* and not the direct form, is shown to be present.

Exercises.

Write the chords indicated by the following figured Basses, and mark the appropriate Roman Numeral:

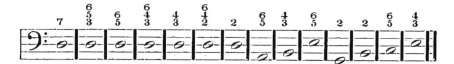

Resolutions of Inversions of the Chord of the Dominant Seventh.

173.   If the simple tendencies shown in § 157 are followed, the pupil will have no difficulty in resolving the inversions of the Chord of the Seventh.   Remember, that the Leading-note tends upward, the 7th from the root downward, Augmented intervals tend to increase, while Diminished intervals contract.   (See §§ 152 to 155.)

Exercises.

(*a.*)   Following the above principles, resolve the

inversions shown in Fig. 51, and place the proper Roman Numeral under each chord.

Fig. 51.

(*b*.)   Write inversions of the chord of the Dominant 7th, and resolve them, in the keys of G: F; D; B♭; A· E♭; B; A♭; F♯.

Exercises.

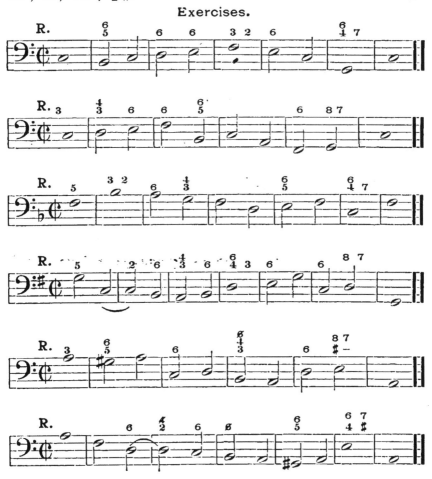

175. Exercises in Harmonizing the Scale.

Harmonize the scales, using the chords of the 7th with their inversions, and the triads with their inversions.

CHAPTER VII.

SECONDARY CHORDS OF THE SEVENTH.

176. The chord of the Dominant Seventh, because it plays such an important part in the key, is also called the *Principal chord of the seventh.** The chords formed upon the remaining degrees (for they are nearly all found in Harmony) are called *Secondary* or *Collateral* Sevenths.

Formation of Secondary Chords of the Seventh.

As seen in §§ 147 and 148, they are formed by the addition of a 7th to the triads upon the various degrees of the scale. As the triads are of various kinds, viz., Major, Minor, Diminished or Augmented, the Secondary seventh-chords will have the same variety of formation,

---

* It is also called the *Fundamental Seventh*, since its intervals are formed like those of Nature's (Harmonic) chord, with Major triad and Minor 7th from a Root-tone. (See § 90.)

thus contrasting with the Dominant Seventh with its
Major 3rd and Minor 7th.

This irregularity of construction should not be considered a fault,
for the chord of the Dominant 7th points so strongly to the Tonic,
that if *all* the Chords of the Seventh were like it the sense of Tonality
would be disturbed. (See § 266.) As it is, the characteristics of the
key are much better preserved than would otherwise be the case.
Again, as we need Major, Minor, Diminished, and Augmented triads
to make up the complete list of triads in a key, so do we need the
same variety in the structure of the Chords of the Seventh.

Resolution of Secondary Chords of the Seventh.

177.   As the Secondary Chords of the 7th are formed
in a manner similar to the chord of the Dominant Seventh,
so their resolution follows in a general way the same pattern; viz., the Chord as a whole tends to resolve to the
Triad situated a 4th higher than the root of the Chord of
the Seventh.   This is the same as from the Dominant
to the Tonic.   (See § 158, foot-note.)   More accurately
expressed, the chord D–F–A–C would tend to resolve to
the triad on G for G is a 4th higher than D. So also
E–G–B–D would resolve to the triad on A, since A is a
4th higher than E.

The individual notes in a Secondary Seventh-chord
have a tendency, though not so pronounced, to progress as
in the Dominant Seventh-chord; viz., the 7th from the
root may descend, and the 3rd from the root may ascend.

Fig. 52.

For example, in Fig. 52 the general tendency is to the
triad on G (the Cadencing Resolution).   The 7th, C,
being a minor 7th and therefore a dissonance with the

root, tends downward; F tends upward, not so much on account of any dissonance or " Influence," as for the reason that it is the shortest way to a place in the next chord and that we are accustomed, in the chord of the Dominant 7th, to hear the corresponding tone pass upward. According to Influence 8, it could also pass downward to D, making the second chord fuller. For many cases this would be better than the upward progression, provided that it made no bad hidden 5ths with the Bass. If the Bass should move upward to G, this would be quite satisfactory; e. g.,

Fig. 53.

Exercises.

178. (*a.*) Form Chords of the 7th upon all degrees of the scale of C Major, and resolve them as shown in Fig. 52, or 53.

NOTE. The resolution of the seventh-chord upon the 4th degree of the scale to the triad upon the 7th degree, is not commonly used, for the following reason :— A Dependent chord demands a resolution to an *Independent* chord. Now, as the triad on the 7th degree is a *Diminished* triad, it is not Independent, and is therefore not suited to be a chord of resolution. But it is possible to use this progression if the triad upon the 7th degree should in its turn be followed by an independent triad; e. g.,

Fig. 54. 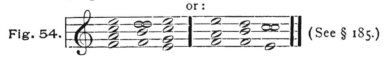 (See § 185.)

Another restriction in the use of the chord of the 7th on the fourth degree of the scale is shown in the foot-note to § 187.

(*b.*) Write the Secondary Seventh-chords with their resolutions in the key of F ; in the key of G ; also of D; B♭; A; E♭; F♯.

Chord of the Seventh upon the 7th Degree in Major.

179. As a Secondary chord of the 7th, the natural resolution of this chord is:

Fig. 55.

This is quite correct. But a more common resolution is found in a consideration of the following :—

We have seen how the Leading-note (7th degree of the scale) has a strong tendency to progress to the Tonic. (See § 152.) The *triad* formed upon this note has also a strong tendency to progress to the Tonic triad (see Fig. 56), resulting from this tendency, while the *chord of the 7th* upon the same note is even more strongly inclined to progress in the same direction. E.g., (play it) ·

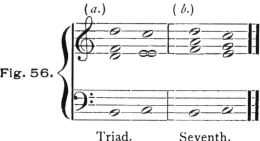

Fig. 56.

Triad.   Seventh.

There are two reasons for this tendency; viz.,

(*a.*) The tendency of the Leading-note, mentioned above.

(*b.*) The similarity of construction to the chord of the Dominant Seventh, which progresses naturally to the Tonic. For example, G–B–D–F (play it) is the chord of the Dominant 7th, resolving to the Tonic triad C–E–G (play it). If now the Root, G, is omitted, we have the triad B–D–F remaining, which resolves just as if the Root were present. This chord without the root (B–D–F), is seen to be the same as the triad formed upon the 7th degree of the scale. Now, as the triad upon the 7th degree has such a distinct tendency toward the Tonic triad, it will be readily understood that the chord of the seventh upon the same degree has a similar tendency, which is increased, rather than diminished, by the addition of the 7th. This similarity to Dominant harmony will be further explained in Chapter IX.

180. From a consideration of the above, it will be seen that the Chord of the Seventh upon the 7th degree may be looked upon in two ways: (*a*) As an incomplete form of Dominant harmony, (in which case it would resolve most naturally to the Tonic triad, as in Fig. 56, *b*) ; or (*b*) As an ordinary Secondary Seventh-chord upon the 7th degree, resolving most naturally to the triad a 4th higher, as in Fig. 55.

Preparation of Dissonant Intervals.

181. A dissonance may be either agreeable or disagreeable. This anomaly is explained by the fact, that although a chord may sound well, it is *technically* called a dissonance if it *demands that another chord should follow* to give a feeling of completion or repose. (See §§ 150 and 151.) It was formerly the rule, that all dissonances should be " prepared." At the present day it is the custom to " prepare " only *harsh* dissonances. The chord of the Dominant seventh was the first to be freed from the restriction, and the chord of the Diminished seventh is also free,* while the Secondary Chords of the Seventh, and the Chord of the Ninth (par-

---

* Though not requiring preparation, it is well to approach the milder dissonances by a *Diatonic step* rather than by a skip.

ticularly the Minor Ninth, because it is a harsh dissonance), are usually prepared. " Preparing " a dissonance
means, that the note which causes the dissonance shall have
been present as a *consonance* in the chord immediately
preceding ; e. g.,

The note C, having appeared in the first chord as a consonant note, is thus " prepared " in the second chord where
it is a dissonant note.

182.   Instead of being " prepared," all dissonant notes
may enter diatonically ; i. e., from the next step above
or below.   E. g.,

(The dissonant note C enters from the next step above.)
In general, therefore, we should not skip to a dissonant
interval, but either " prepare " it or lead stepwise into it.

183.   A dissonant note, i. e., a note which forms a
dissonance with another, should not be doubled.   Being
a tendency-note, as all dissonances are, if it were to be
doubled either consecutive 8ves would result, or a contradiction of its natural tendency by one of the notes.   (See
§ 162.)

184.   Exercises.

Succession of Chords of the Seventh ; Resolution of one Seventh-Chord to another Seventh-Chord.

185.   Instead of resolving to a triad, as shown in the preceding chapters, a Chord of the Seventh may progress to another Seventh-Chord; e. g.,

Fig. 57.

II^7 V^7

Fig. 57 might be called a contraction of Fig. 58; for,

Fig. 58.

II^7 V V^7

since the Chord of the Seventh is merely an enlargement of a triad (see § 147), we are allowed to progress directly from one Seventh-Chord to another, considering that the Tonic Triad, or regular resolution, is implied in its enlarged form.

Advanced Course.

See "How to Modulate," page 42.

Regular Course.

186.   Exercises.

Secondary Sevenths in Minor.

Advanced Course.

Exercises.

187. (*a.*) As in § 148, the pupil will form Seventh-Chords upon each degree of the scale of C Minor, and describe them.

He will notice that some of these Seventh-Chords, like the triads of the Minor scale, are too harsh for practical use, owing to the various extremely dissonant intervals contained. It will be noticed that, beside the Dominant Seventh (*which is alike in Major and Minor*), the most agreeable of the Secondary Chords of the Seventh in Minor are those upon the 2nd and 7th degrees. The others, either on account of their harshness or the forced leading of the parts in their resolution, are but seldom used.

(*b.*) The pupil should try to resolve the Seventh-Chord upon each degree of the minor scale — i. e., the Cadencing resolution to the triad a 4th higher — and he will see the difficulty of resolving some of them without bad leading of the parts.*

---

* The pupil will find, in resolving the seventh-chord upon the 4th degree, that the Bass, if moving *upward* to its note of resolution, passes over the interval of three whole steps, an awkward skip called the Tritone, which is forbidden. It may progress downward to the octave of the same note without hindrance. Being comparatively ill adapted for singing, like the step of the Augmented 2nd, the Tritone is not to be used for the present. (See § 329.)

188.   It will be observed that the chord upon the 7th degree, though a very agreeable chord, does not resolve well to the Augmented triad a 4th higher, but rather inclines to the triad upon the 1st degree.   In this it is seen to correspond with the same chord in Major, i. e., the Chord of the Seventh upon the 7th degree (see § 179), and is explained in the same manner, viz., by the strong tendency of the 7th degree of the scale, or Leading-note, toward the Tonic.   Fig. 59 illustrates the chord of the seventh upon the 7th degree in minor, with the resolution to the tonic as described above.   The interval B–A♭ is a Diminished 7th, and from this interval the chord is named the chord of the *Diminished Seventh*.   It will be further explained in Chapter IX.

Fig. 59.

Exercises.

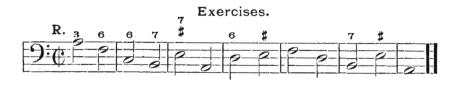

Inversions of Secondary Chords of the Seventh.

Regular Course.

189.   In §172 the pupil learned to form Chords of the Seventh upon every degree of the scale, also to invert and figure them.

In the following exercises, containing inversions of the Secondary Chords of the Seventh, no new points are to be considered. Attention to the principles of Influences and Tendencies will guide the pupil here as in *all other chords*.

Exercises.

Cadences: Closing Formula.

190. It has been remarked that the succession of the Chord of the Dominant 7th and the Tonic triad, which gives such a feeling of a close, is called a Cadence, or Cadencing Resolution, also called the Authentic Cadence.

There are various forms of ending a musical thought more or less elaborate and of varying character as regards the decisiveness of the close. In ordinary cadences the Tonic chord occurs upon an accented part of the measure (*thesis*), and the Dominant Seventh on an unaccented part (*arsis.*)

These various Cadences are named and defined as follows :—

Perfect Cadence. The most absolute close : both the Soprano and Bass of the last (Tonic) triad sound the Root of the chord. (Ex. *a*, Fig. 60.)

Imperfect Cadence. Not so decisive as the first : either the Soprano or Bass does not sound the root of the Tonic (closing) triad. (Ex. *b*, Fig. 60.)

Plagal Cadence. Where the final chord is preceded by the triad on the Subdominant instead of the Dominant · an old church-form. (Ex. *c*, Fig. 60.)

Half-Close. Where the Dominant follows the Tonic instead of preceding it. (Ex. *d*, Fig. 60.)

Deceptive Cadence. Where the Dominant Seventh-chord, instead of resolving to the Tonic triad, progresses to the triad on some other degree of the scale, thus disappointing and deceiving the natural expectation that it will resolve to the Tonic. (Ex. *e*, Fig. 60. See § 192.)

Modulatory False (Deceptive) **Cadence.** Where the Dominant Seventh-chord, instead of resolving to the Tonic triad, progresses to a chord in a foreign key, thus producing a modulation. This will be further explained in § 195. (Ex. *ƒ*, Fig. 60.)

Fig. 60.

Exercises.

(*a.*) Return to the exercises in §§ 170, 173 and 174, and describe the cadences formed by the resolution of the chords of the 7th.

Closing Formula.

191. A more extended form of close, which includes the Cadencing resolution shown above, is called the Closing Formula. It will be seen that not only does the chord of the Dominant 7th point directly to the close, but that there is a distinct impression in the preceding chords. Many changes can be made in the succession of chords constituting the Closing Formula, there being no rule as to their order.

A few of the more common forms are —

(*a.*) IV, V^7, I.
(*b.*) IV, I^6_4, V^7, I.
(*c.*) II, V^7, I.
(*d.*) IV, II, V^7, I. Play them.

The Closing Formula is useful in giving a sense of close at the end of a phrase, or in establishing a key after a modulation. (See § 289.)

Non-Cadencing Resolutions of the Chord of the Seventh.

192. The resolution of the Dominant seventh-chord to the Tonic triad has been shown as the most natural progression. There are many other resolutions possible,

which are called *non-cadencing* resolutions, for the reason that the Chord of the Seventh does not move in the
manner of a Cadencing Resolution to the triad a 4th
higher (i. e., the Tonic triad), but progresses to the
triad upon some other degree of the scale, or even to a
chord in another key.   Non-cadencing resolutions are
useful in composition when it is desired to employ the
chord of the Dominant 7th and still avoid a close which
is so plainly indicated by the use of the Dominant 7th
followed by the Tonic triad.

Among these Non-cadencing resolutions are the
Deceptive Cadence and the *Modulatory False Cadence*,
both of which are classed among the cadences (§ 190) by
name only, not being *true* Cadences.

In Non-cadencing resolutions the Tendencies and
Influences are in a somewhat greater degree disregarded,
the progressions consequently being usually rather unnatural, and in some cases quite forced.   But if we were
to use only the simplest and most natural progressions,
the variety of effects would be very limited.   It will be
observed that in the Non-cadencing resolutions the dissonant intervals do not always resolve to the nearest consonances.

193.   As the pupil, after studying the use of the common note in connecting two triads (102), at once learned how to connect two triads
without that common note, thus enlarging his powers, so here, after
learning the natural resolution of the chord of the 7th, the pupil finds
enlarged possibilities in the management of these chords by the use
of the Non-cadencing resolutions.   They should be understood not as
contradictions, but as enlarged liberties in the treatment of the Chord
of the Seventh, for instead of forcing the Chord of the Seventh
always to resolve to the Tonic, it is allowed, so to speak, to
mingle with a larger circle, or to progress to triads upon other
degrees of the scale, or in other keys.   This gives it a freedom
similar to that of the triads, which are at liberty to progress not only to
other triads having a common note, but also to nearly all others which

can be reached without bad leading of the parts. Many of these progressions should not be called resolutions, since the Tendencies and Influences are disregarded, but should rather be called *connections*, being connected with the following chord in the same manner as the triads. Indeed, it should not be forgotten that Chords of the 7th are merely Triads with one or more notes added, and therefore they may easily be expected to retain the properties and privileges of triads.

Exercises.

194.   Below are given examples of Non-cadencing resolutions and connections.   Analyze them, pointing out the unnatural progressions of the dissonant intervals, and, if possible, giving the reason.   It will be noticed that the 7th is frequently stationary, or even progresses upward, thus giving the effect of a connection or progression from chord to chord, rather than the resolution of a dissonance. When the Tendencies and Influences are disregarded, especial care must be taken not to violate the rules of correct part-leading.

Fig. 61.

The possible combinations with the Non-cadencing resolutions of the Chords of the Seventh are almost limitless, as will be shown in the next exercises. The above examples marked N. B. show the connection of the Dominant seventh-chord with the Dominant seventh-chords of various foreign keys: such connections will be further explained in the chapter on Modulation.

Exercises.

Advanced Course.

195. Non-cadencing Connections with Triads in the Key.

(*a.*) Starting upon the Chord of the Dominant 7th in the key of C, try to resolve it to (or connect with) the triad upon each degree of the key of C. If the effect is not good, try a change of position in the first chord; if the different leading of the parts does not produce an agreeable effect, reject the triad and try the next one.

(*b.*) Repeat in various keys.

Non-cadencing Connections with Triads Foreign to the Key.

(*c.*) Starting upon the Chord of the Dominant 7th in the key of C, try to connect it with the Major triad upon each degree of the Chromatic scale. Reject the unsatisfactory progressions.

(*d.*) Try to connect the Chord of the Dominant 7th in C with the *Minor* triad upon each degree of the Chromatic scale, as above.

(*e.*) Starting upon the Dominant Seventh-Chord in other keys, try to connect with the Major and Minor triads as before, rejecting all progressions that cannot be made effective.

Non-cadencing Connections with Dominant Seventh-Chords in Foreign Keys.

(*f.*) Starting upon the chord of the Dominant 7th in C, try to connect it with the chord of the Dominant 7th in all other keys (proceeding Chromatically as before).

(*g.*) Starting upon the chord of the Dominant 7th in other keys, try to connect with all other chords of the Dominant 7th as above.

In the above exercises it will be found that those connections are best which have a note common to both chords, and that few connections can be made without it.

The exercises at (*f*) and (*g*) will be treated further in Chapter XIII.

196. Exercises.

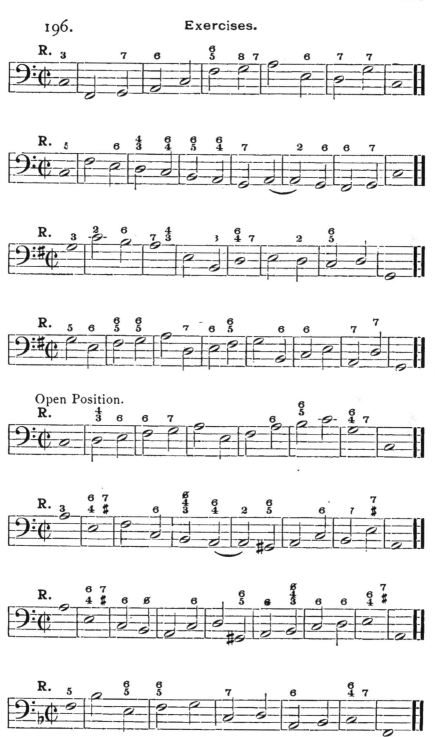

Non-Cadencing Connections of Secondary Chords of the Seventh.

197. We have seen how the Chords of the Dominant Seventh are frequently connected with chords other than those forming the Cadencing resolution.

The Secondary Chords of the Seventh are capable of being treated in a similar manner. Many of them especially in Minor, which cannot be used in the Cadeucing resolution, may be connected with other chords with very good effect. As in the free resolution of the Dominant Seventh-chord, the 7th from the root may progress downward, remain stationary, or progress upward, as desired.

Exercises.

198. (*a.*) Try in succession the Secondary Seventh-Chords in the key of C major, and find as many agreeable connections with other chords as possible (even connecting with chords in other keys), proceeding in detail as shown in § 195.

(*b.*) Proceed similarly with the Secondary Seventh-Chords in C minor ; also in other keys.

Rules for Figured Bass.

199. Short horizontal lines following figures denote the retention.in the following chord, or continuation, of the notes indicated by the figures. E. g., the notes indicated by 6 and by 3 are continued into the following chord. In notes, thus : —

Even when the Bass note changes, the horizontal lines denote the continuance of the notes already sounding, whether indicated by figures in the preceding chord or not; e. g.,

Analytical and Comparative Review.

201. The pupil should strive to keep his knowledge collected and classified. To this end it is desirable to tabulate some of the facts already learned, the student being expected to find the definitions and commit them to memory if he is not already familiar with them.

(1.) *How the terms* Major, Minor, Augmented, and Diminished *are used.*

I.   Intervals :—
      there are —
II.   Triads :—   } Major, Minor, Augmented, Diminished.
      there are —

III.   Chords of the
      Seventh :—   } Major, Minor, Diminished.
      the 7th may be—

(2.) *How the term* Principal *is used:—*

I. Triads: — Tonic, subdominant, and Dominant

II. Chords of the Seventh: — Dominant.

(3.) *How the term* Secondary *is used:—*

I. Triads: — Upon all degrees not occupied by Principal triads.

II. Chords of the Seventh:— Upon all degrees not occupied by Principal Seventh.

(4.) *Of Tendencies:—*

Melodic:—
I. Of Leading-note — to the Tonic.
II. Of the Third — upward.
III. Of the Fourth — downward.
IV. Of Continuity — to continue in either direction.
V. Of an accidental Sharp —to ascend.
VI. Of an accidental Flat — to descend.

Harmonic:—
I. Of a Diminished Interval;— to become still less.
II. Of an Augmented Interval;— to become still greater.

(5.) *Natural Resolutions:—*

I. Of Dominant Seventh;— to triad a 4th higher, i. e., the Tonic.

II. Of Secondary Sevenths;—to triad a 4th higher

III. Of Seventh-Chord on 7th degree;— to Tonic or to triad a 4th higher.

(6.) *Non-Cadencing Resolutions:—*

I. Of Dominant Seventh;— to secondary triads in the key.

II. Of Dominant Seventh;— to foreign chords.

III. Of Secondary Sevenths;— to various triads in the key.

IV. Of Secondary Sevenths;— to foreign chords.

(7.) *Figuring Inversions :—*

I. Of Triads ; — According to distance from actual Bass.

II. Of Chords of the Seventh ; — Same as triads.

Synopsis.

Write the usual Synopsis of the chapter.

Historical.

Concluded from page 39.

Triads and Chords of the Seventh.

202. With Palestrina (early in the 16th century) the Harmonic effects began, though unconsciously, to appear upon the horizon of musical development. First the Common chord was used in its direct form, then with its inversions. Next we find the alternation of consonances and dissonances, and after a time Suspensions and Reso lutions. The use of the Chord of the Seventh (Dominant seventh) met with much opposition at first. For many years its dissonant notes were " prepared," but in recent times gradually increasing freedom has been allowed, until now the chord can be used without especial caution. Following in the path of the Chord of the Seventh came the Chords of the Ninth, the Chord of the Diminished Seventh, and the chords of the Augmented Sixth (to be described in subsequent chapters), all of which have been shown to be various forms of Dominant (or Dependent) harmony. Afterward came the various forms of ornaments, and devices for imparting variety, shown in Part III.

The development of the Harmonic System, and of the modern scale as opposed to the Gregorian Modes, were to a great extent coincident and mutually dependent; for, whereas the Gregorian Modes were formed in reference to the Melody, the modern scale was designed with direct reference to the requirements of chord-construction. (See § 46.)

This brings the history to the close of the 16th century, when it was substantially as it is to-day. The boundaries of the keys had been well defined, and the use of the more ordinary chords had become common. Since then more freedom in the use of the Dependent chords has been gained, and a knowledge of those closely related chords which lie just beyond the limits of a key, but are used as if they belonged to it. (See Chap. XII.) During the last two centuries progress has been more in the line of development than of discovery.

(End of Historical Remarks.)

The Perceptive Faculties.

203 The teacher will not need further detailed instructions, as the same manner of hearing the tones individually, of singing them by syllable, of writing them, and hearing them collectively, is here followed. The teacher should be careful to grade his instruction in this department well within the abilities of the pupil, and to proceed very slowly. Exercises in Rhythm, and in Altered intervals (Aug. and Dim.), may properly be introduced or continued at this period.

CHAPTER VIII.

THE CHORD OF THE DOMINANT SEVENTH AND NINTH.

204. The formation of chords has been repeatedly shown to be a process of building, or adding to a Root or Fundamental note. (See §§ 90 and 147.) It has also

been noticed that each note added is at the interval of a 3rd from the next lower note.

If, according to this plan, a note be added to the Chord of the Seventh, there will be produced a chord of the Seventh and Ninth, called also the chord of the Ninth. As the one most commonly used is derived from the Dominant, we will consider only that one at present. In Fig. 62 is shown, at (*a*), the chord of the Seventh, and at (*b*) the same with the 9th added.

Fig. 62.

In a Major key the 9th will be Major; and in a Minor key the 9th will be Minor, as shown in Fig. 63; the 9th, A, being made flat by the signature.

Fig. 63.

The pupil should not look upon this as a new and strange chord, but as a Chord of the Dominant Seventh with an interval added. The Chord of the Seventh was produced by adding a note to the triad, and the Chord of the Ninth is formed by a further addition of a note to the chord of the Seventh.

205. The characteristics of the chord (the dissonant intervals and the Tendencies) *are not changed by add-ing the new interval*, as may be seen by tracing the dissonant intervals in the same manner as shown in § 157. It is apparent that the added note merely creates two new dissonant intervals, the 9th from the root, and the 7th from B.* As both these intervals would be re-

---

* In the chord of the Minor Ninth there is also the dissonant interval of a Diminished 5th, D-A♭, in Fig. 63.

solved by allowing the 9th, A, to descend in the resolution of the chord, it is apparent that the addition of the new interval *does not alter the natural resolution of the underlying chord of the 7th*, or in any way change its nature. We merely need to be careful to avoid consecutive 5ths, which may occur in adding the new note. The Tendencies of the various notes and intervals are not changed. Therefore, the chord of the Dominant Seventh and Ninth is seen to be *only an enlarged form of Dominant Harmony.*

206. Fig. 64 illustrates the resolution of the chord of the Dominant seventh and ninth according to the above, the first chord being used to prepare the dissonance (see § 181), which is particularly harsh when entering abruptly. As there are *five* notes in this chord, *one* must be omitted in four-part writing. The 5th, being the least essential and characteristic, and also the tone with which the ninth might create consecutive 5ths, is usually the one left out.

Fig. 64.

Exercises.

207. From the chord of the Dominant Seventh in every key, both Major and Minor, form the chord of the Seventh and Ninth; find and describe their dissonances and Tendencies as shown in § 157; prepare and resolve them as shown in Fig. 64.

The consideration of the above is of great importance and should be thoroughly understood, as the following chapters are derived directly from this section.

Inversions and Figuring.

208.   The inversions of this chord are used, excepting those in which the root and the 9th come too close together.   The figuring is similar to that of the Chords of the Seventh, the added note simply adding a figure.

Exercises.

Form examples of inversions of the Chord of the seventh and ninth.

Secondary Chords of the Seventh and Ninth.

209.   Secondary chords of the Seventh and Ninth are occasionally used, though not often.   Not belonging to Dominant harmony, the 9th and the 7th (the dissonant intervals) must both be prepared.   In the Dominant Seventh and Ninth-Chord the preparation is not obligatory, though customary.

Synopsis.

Write the usual synopsis of the chapter.

———

CHAPTER IX.

THE CHORD OF THE DIMINISHED SEVENTH.

210.   The Chord of the Seventh upon the 7th degree in Major has already been mentioned as partaking of the qualities of Dominant harmony (§179).   The Chord of the Seventh upon the 7th degree in Minor partakes of these qualities in a still more marked degree.   (See § 188.)   They are both considered as incomplete forms of Dominant harmony.   The one formed upon the 7th

degree in Minor is especially important, as it occurs very frequently, gives a smooth effect without being prepared, and is of great value in modulations. (See § 300.)

Construction of the Chord of the Diminished Seventh.

211. This chord is derived from the Chord of the Dominant Seventh and Ninth in the Minor mode, by simply *omitting the root.*

Fig. 65.

In Fig. 65 at (*a*) is given the Chord of the Dominant 7th and 9th as shown in Fig. 63. If the root is omitted, we have the chord shown at (*b*), Fig 65, which is a chord of the Diminished Seventh, but it is *considered as derived from the root G* (indicated in Fig. 65 by w·), and therefore having the *same resolution as if the root were actually present.* Therefore we say that the chord of the *Diminished Seventh is an incomplete form of Dominant harmony.*

In the chord of the Dominant 7th and 9th the dissonant intervals are the Minor 7th from the root and the Minor 9th. In the chord of the Diminished Seventh, the *same notes*, F and A♭, *form the dissonances*, appearing as a Diminished 5th and a Diminished 7th from the Bass of the chord. These dissonances are resolved in the same manner as if the root were also sounding, e. g.,

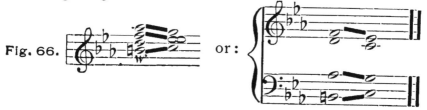

Fig. 66.   or :

Exercises.

212. (1) Form Chords of the Minor 7th and 9th upon all notes from C to C, i. e., upon C, C♯, D, D♯, etc; also using flats instead of sharps, as D♭ for C♯, E♭ for D♯, etc.

(2) From each chord of the Minor 9th just written, form a chord of the Diminished 7th by omitting the root and writing the sign ⋎' in its place.

(3) Resolve each chord of the Diminished 7th according to the tendencies in § 157. N. B. It will be found that the resolution is the same as if the root were still sounding; see Fig. 64.

Use of the Chord of the Diminished Seventh in Major Keys.

213. In § 204 it was apparent that the Chord of the 9th is Major in Major keys, and Minor in Minor keys. The Chord of the Minor 9th and its derivative, the Chord of the Diminished 7th, are, however, often used in Major keys, the 9th from the root being lowered by an accidental; e. g.,

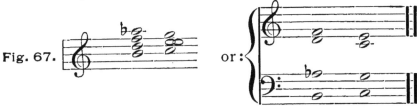

Fig. 67.

As the Chord of the Dominant *Seventh* is alike in Major and Minor, we may say that it resolves equally well to Major or Minor triads; and the same holds good of *all* forms of Dominant harmony, whether Chords of the 7th, of the 7th and 9th, or of the Diminished 7th.

Exercises.

214. (1) From the Chord of the Dominant 7th, in all major keys, form Chords of the Major 9th as shown

in Fig. 62. From these chords of the Major 9th form chords of the Minor 9th by lowering the Ninth by an accidental. Omit the root of the Minor ninth-chords, producing Chords of the Diminished 7th in Major.

(2) Resolve these chords of the Diminished 7th as in Fig. 66 or 67. N. B. The chord of the Diminished 7th resolves to either a Major or a Minor triad, as mentioned in § 213.

Similarity of Sound of the Diminished Seventh-Chords.

215. Write the chords of the Diminished Seventh as in Fig. 68.* Now play them upon the piano, and it will be seen that there are apparently but three different chords, if we consider that inverting and changing the notation do not alter the sound. This is shown in Fig. 68, where the chords are divided into four groups, *w*, *x*, *y*, *z*; and, by trying at the Piano, it will be seen that No. 1 of group *w* is the same as No. 1 of group *x*, or *y*, or *z*, in that the same notes are struck on the keyboard. The difference consists in the fact that the chord is inverted and differently written. Therefore, any chord of the Diminished Seventh can, by changing its notation, belong to four different keys. This subject will be explained further in § 300.

Fig. 68.

Roots:	G	G♯	A	A♯	B	C	C♯	D	D♯	E	F	F♯
Keys:	C	C♯	D	D♯	E	F	F♯	G	G♯	A	B♭	B
	1	2	3	1	2	3	1	2	3	1	2	3

---

* The pupil should write a series (Chromatic) to represent the roots of the chords, as shown in the line marked " Roots " in Fig. 68 and try to build the required chords from these roots (as shown in § 212) without referring to Fig. 68 unless necessary.

The chord of the Diminished 7th, being Dominant harmony, does not require preparation.

Inversions and Figuring.

216.　The chord of the Diminished 7th is used in all inversions, which are figured by counting from the actual Bass note, as for other chords.　The sign ° is used to indicate Diminished.

Exercises.

(*a*.)　Form a series of Diminished seventh-chords similar to that shown in Fig. 68, but with the sharps changed to flats ; e. g., instead of using F♯ for the Root of a chord, write it G♭, which will cause the whole chord to appear without sharps.　Divide the series into groups as shown in Fig. 68, and number them.　Write also the Roots and Keys under the chords as there shown.

217.　It will now be observed, that by changing the notation of the Root (i. e., from a sharp to a flat, or vice versa), the notation of the whole chord is changed, although the notes on the keyboard remain the same.

218.　It will also be seen,— the first chord of each group (see Fig. 68) being the same,— that, by a change of Root (and therefore of notation), the same chord (i. e., upon the keyboard) may become Dominant harmony in four different keys, as shown by the series of keys in Fig. 68.　As Dominant harmony resolves naturally to its Tonic, it is clear that by proper notation these chords of the Diminished seventh can resolve to any one of four different keys.

Exercises.

219.　(*b*.)　Completing Fig. 68 as required in the foot-note, § 215, take the first chord of *each* group in Fig. 68, and resolve it to its proper Tonic triad as indicated by the notation.

(*c.*) Take the second chord of each group, and proceed as before.

(*d.*) Take the third chord of each group, and proceed as before.

(*e.*) Name the Root of the Diminished seventh-chord which shall resolve to the triad of · D major. (N. B. The *Root* of the chord is desired, not the Bass note. Remember that the Root of the chord of the diminished seventh is the same as the Root of the Dominant harmony from which it is derived; therefore, to find the Root of a chord of the Diminished seventh, the pupil may proceed as in § 159, and, having the Root, the chord may be developed as shown in § 212.) Write the chord, and indicate the root by the proper sign.

(*f.*) Name the Root, and write the chord which shall resolve to the triad of D minor; of A♭ major; of A♭ minor; of F♯; of G♯; of A♯; of B♯; of B♭; of D♭; of E♭.

220.   Exercises.

Exercises in Harmonizing the Scale.

221. Harmonize the scales, using chords of the Diminished seventh where possible, together with the chords previously learned.

Synopsis.

Write the usual synopsis of the chapter.

CHAPTER X.

CHORDS OF THE AUGMENTED SIXTH.

222. Most decided differences of opinion still exist with regard to these chords. They will here be shown to be forms of Dominant harmony, or derived directly from it. This exposition will be found by far the simplest and most practical, giving a more intelligible derivation, and a wider application, than is possible in any other way.*

223. The chords of the Augmented Sixth are Chromatically Altered chords, i. e., chords in which some note has been changed without radically modifying the chord or its progression. (See § 246.)

As the Chords of the Dominant Seventh, the Dominant 7th and 9th, and the Diminished 7th, belong to Dominant harmony, though each appears in a different form (one note more or less; with the Root or without it; etc.), so the chords of the Augmented Sixth are no exception, but may be developed from Dominant harmony, as will be shown.

Construction and Resolution.

224. These harmonies appear in three forms, viz., Augmented Six-Three, Augmented Six-Four-Three, and Augmented Six-Five-Three chords, e. g.,

Fig. 69.

To Construct the Augmented Six-Three Chord.

225. Let us take a Dominant seventh-chord, for example : , place it in its 2nd inversion, ,

---

* Although the full application of the theories here advanced is original with the author, there is abundant authority to support his views. The investigations of the last half-century seem to converge, but the results of research had not yet been systematized and the practical application shown. While not claiming the discovery of new principles, it is here attempted to arrange and apply the truths brought out by Day, Ouseley, MacFarren, Parry, Piutti and other theorists.

omit the Root, 𝄞, and Chromatically lower the 5th from the original Root, giving the chord: 𝄞.
This is called the Chord of the Augmented Six-Three.

The Root being G, and the original chord an ordinary Dominant 7th, the natural resolution is to the triad on C: 𝄞 *just as it would be if the note D were not altered.*

Notice that the Leading-note progresses upward, the Minor 7th downward (as in the ordinary progression of a Dominant 7th chord), and that the interval of an Augmented 4th is resolved naturally by further expansion, as in chords of the Dominant 7th, Diminished 7th, and Minor 9th; while the 5th lowered by an accidental follows the natural tendency downward. The characteristic interval of the Augmented 6th, D♭–B, from which the chord is named, resolves by further expansion.

Exercises.

Taking in turn the chord of the Dominant 7th in every key, place it in its second inversion, omit the Root, lower the 5th (from the Root) by an accidental, thus forming a chord of the Augmented Six-Three, and resolve it as shown above.

To Construct the Augmented Six-Four-Three Chord.

226. If the same Dominant seventh-chord is taken in its second inversion as before, but this time without omitting the Root, and the 5th lowered as above, we shall have the same Augmented Sixth-chord as before, with the addition of the Root, G: . This is called

the Chord of the Augmented Six-Four-Three. For precisely the same reasons as the Augmented Six-Three
chord, the natural resolution is to the triad on C·

Exercises.

Taking in turn the chord of the Dominant 7th in
every key, place it in its second inversion, *not* omitting
the Root, lower the 5th (from the Root), thus forming
a chord of the Augmented Six-Four-Three, and resolve
it as shown above.

To Construct the Augmented Six-Five-Three Chord.

227. If we take the same Dominant harmony as before, this time with the *Minor 9th from the Root added*,

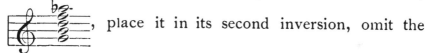, place it in its second inversion, omit the

Root, and lower the 5th (from the Root) by an acci-

dental, we shall have the chord: , called the

Augmented Six-Five, which has the characteristic of sounding like a Dominant seventh-chord. This chord, being
derived from the same harmony as before, though in a
fuller form, has the same natural resolution to the triad

on C:  ·

But here are consecutive 5ths, which may be avoided
in various ways. Among them may be mentioned: (*a*)
Resolving first to an Augmented $\frac{6}{4}$ or $\frac{6}{3}$, which, being precisely the same harmony, does not affect the character of
the final resolution: or (*b*) delaying the resolution of

some of the parts, thus forming a chord of the $\frac{6}{4}$ on the Tonic before the common chord enters. Both ways are exemplified in Fig. 70.

Fig. 70.

Exercises.

Taking in turn the chord of the Dominant 7th in every key, add the Minor 9th, place it in its second inversion, omit the Root, lower the 5th (from the Root) by an accidental, thus forming a chord of the Augmented Six-Five-Three, and resolve it as above

228. The chord of the Augmented Six-Three is called the Italian Sixth; the chord of the Augmented Six-Four-Three is called the French Sixth; and the chord of the Augmented Six-Five-Three is called the German Sixth. These names are given with reference to the nations which (supposedly) first used them.

In the Italian Sixth, there being but three notes, it is necessary to double one of them. The best one to double is the 7th from the *true* Root. (N. B. It is quite proper in this case to double the 7th, since by the omission of the Root the downward tendency of the 7th is less marked than if it were present.)

Another reason is, that the lowering of another note by an accidental disturbs the feeling of Tonality, so that the 7th does not seem to have the full tendency downward. (See " How to Modulate," §§ 44 and 45.) The tendencies thus having been removed or modified, can hardly be said to have been violated.

N. B. The pupil should now review chapters V to

X, especially comparing §§ 157, 173, 177, 179, 180, 205, 211, and 224—228. He must not fail to understand practically that, as asserted, **the Chords of the Dominant 7th, Diminished 7th, Major and Minor 9th, and the three forms of the Chord of the Augmented 6th, are nothing more than different forms of the same Fundamental harmony, derived from the same Root, having the same dissonant intervals, and the same resolution.**

Note. All chords of the Augmented sixth are properly classed among the Altered chords. (See Chapter XI.)

Chord of the Augmented Sixth derived from the Supertonic.

229. There is another chord of the Augmented Sixth, which, although it is not strictly in the key, is in such common use that it will be mentioned here.

The chord in question is the one which resolves to the Chord on the Dominant. Therefore, its Root should be found a 4th lower than the Dominant, i. e., on the Supertonic. In order to have exactly the form of a Dominant seventh and ninth-chord (which must be exact in all its intervals if it is to serve as the basis of an Augmented Sixth-Chord), the 3rd from the Root must be Major. Therefore, in Fig. 71, F must be made sharp, though the signature does not require it. The Minor 9th from D, which is necessary for the Six-Five form, is E♭, which also is not indicated by the signature. Thus this chord is not so strictly in the key as are the above examples.

Taking this chord as the basis, by placing it in its second inversion and lowering the 5th from the original Root, which Root is to be omitted (remember that the Root is D), we shall have a Chord of the Augmented Sixth, which resolves to the Dominant.

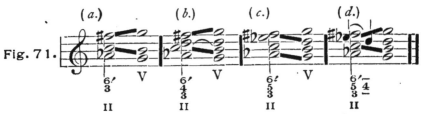

Fig. 71.

In Fig. 71 are shown the various forms of $\frac{6}{3}$, $\frac{6}{4}$, and $\frac{6}{3}$, at (*a*), (*b*) and (*c*). The consecutive 5ths at (*c*) may be avoided as shown in (*d*), and as mentioned in § 227.

230. This chord was discovered and used before the one derived from the Dominant (Fig. 69), and was long considered the only one in the key. But, as just seen, it is not so strictly in the key as the one derived from the Dominant, as there are no less than three altered notes in the Six-Five form, and two altered notes in the other forms. (For further explanation of Augmented Sixth-Chords see " How to Modulate, " Chapter V.)

Exercises.

231. Form chords of the Augmented Sixth (in three forms) upon the Supertonic of all keys, and resolve them to their Dominant triads as shown in Fig. 71.

The pupil must not fail to follow the process given in § 229, of starting from a given Root, building the chord of the 7th (or 7th and 9th, as may be required,) not forgetting that the 3rd from the root is to be raised by an accidental, placing it in its second inversion, omitting the root or not as required, and lowering the 5th from original root. Careless pupils try to jump at conclusions, and often end in knowing but little of their subject.

232.   **Exercises.**

233. Sometimes the Augmented Sixth-Chord upon the Supertonic, instead of resolving directly to the Dominant, progresses to the Tonic Six-Four Chord, which is thus interposed between the Augmented Sixth and its natural resolution, the Dominant. This is the case at the points marked N. B. in the second and third exercises in § 232.

Exercises in Harmonizing the Scale.

Harmonize the scales, using chords of the Augmented 6th where possible, together with all the chords previously learned.

Exercises.

234. Compare the formation of the different chords with each other as shown in § 228, and, taking any note for a Root, try to develop the different chords from that Root.

Synopsis.

Write the usual synopsis of the chapter.

Recapitulation.

235. It cannot be too strongly impressed, that the whole harmonic system is a process of building from a Fundamental, or Root. From the Prime tone is developed the triad, by adding a 3rd and 5th. The Chord of the Seventh is formed by the addition of another note; and the Chord of the Ninth by still another. The chord of the Diminished Seventh is formed from the Chord of the Minor Ninth by the omission of the Root. The Chord of the Augmented Sixth is formed by inverting the Chord of the Minor Ninth and Chromatically Altering the 5th from the Root. *Thus the triad is the foundation of all chords.*

The following *Synopsis of Chords* shows this in detail.

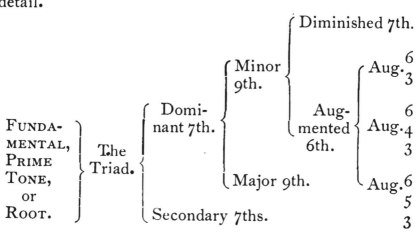

236. It will be further observed that-

(a.) The natural resolution of all Dependent chords is governed by the same Tendencies and Influences.

(b.) The same laws of Part-leading control the connection of all chords, Independent or Dependent.

(c.) Dependent chords may sometimes progress without cadencing resolution, in which case they are governed, not by the laws of natural resolution, but by the laws of part-leading in chord-connections as in Independent chords.

237. From a consideration of the above it will be seen, that the different chords are but different forms or manifestations of the same Primary chord. It is, therefore, but logical that, as above shown, the same laws should govern all the forms. The Harmonic System is wonderfully simple, yet complete.

CHAPTER XI.

ALTERED CHORDS: FUNDAMENTAL CHORDS.

How to Distinguish them; Their Roots and Keys.

238. Any note of a chord may be Chromatically raised or lowered; e. g.,

When this occurs, certain changes take place which render it necessary to consider the chord from a new point of view. To enable the pupil to understand the changes which take place, it is necessary to study the following.

Preliminary Premises.

239. (1.) Fundamental chords (i. e. chords like Dominant chords, also like Nature's chord), can be built upon any and every note. (See § 91.) Funda mental chords may appear as triads, Chords of the 7th, of the Diminished 7th, of the Major 9th, or the Minor 9th. They must have, counting from the Root, a Major 3rd, a Perfect 5th, a Minor 7th (if a chord of the 7th), and a Major or a Minor 9th (if a chord of the 9th). Or, for convenience in comparing, the chord may be described by describing the successive 3rds when the chord is in its Direct form, as follows:—

From 1 to 3 is a Major 3rd, from 3 to 5 is a Minor 3rd, from 5 to 7 is a Minor 3rd, and from 7 to 9 is either a Major or a Minor 3rd according to the key. Placed one above the other as in the chord, it may be expressed as follows:—*

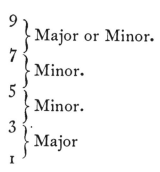

This might be called the Formula for constructing Fundamental chords, since they must correspond exactly with it in order to be Fundamental.

Exercises.

240. Form Fundamental chords in the four forms mentioned, upon all notes of the Chromatic scale, and compare them with the formula.

241. (2.) Fundamental Dependent chords, like Dominant chords, whether appearing as Chords of the 7th, Diminished 7th, or of the 9th, resolve naturally to the triad a 4th higher. (See foot-note, § 158.)

242. (3.) All Fundamental chords are considered as built, each upon a particular Root. The chord of resolution is a 4th higher than this Root, in every case.

243. (4.) *Change of Root.* This can best be explained by illustration. By reference to § 241, it becomes apparent that the natural resolution of any dependent chord is to the triad a 4th higher.

Reference to Fig. 68 and the accompanying text shows that the same notes (on the keyboard) may be

---

* If the Root is omitted, as in the chord of the Diminished seventh, the Major 3rd from 1 to 3 will not be present in the formula.

derived from different Root-notes, the only difference being in the manner of writing the chords, i. e., the notation.

It may be said, conversely, that the *different nota-*
tion shows that the chords spring 'from different
Roots. To illustrate, (*a*) and (*b*) of Fig. 72 are
alike in sound. But, if a chord of the Diminished 7th

Fig. 72.

is built upon the Root G, it will be like (*a*), while a
similar chord erected upon the Root A♯ will be like (*b*)
when inverted. The two chords, which sound alike,
have different notation *because they are erected upon*
different Roots. Reference to § 211 will show that
their resolutions differ radically. This is on account of
the law of Tendencies shown in § 152, viz., the Leading-
note tends toward the Tonic, the fourth degree of the
scale tends downward, and the chief dissonance, the Diminished 7th between the Leading-note and the 9th from
the original Root, tends to contract. Therefore we may
say that, by the change of notation, the Root is changed,
and, consequently, the resolution is also changed.

Therefore, if we would have a proper resolution
the chord must be *so written as to show which note is*
the Leading-note, which the 9th from the original
Root, etc., in order to know how to apply the law of
Tendencies.

244. In § 243 is shown how a change of notation,
or Enharmonic change, as it is called, implies a change
of Root, even where the notes on the keyboard remain
the same. In cases where one or more notes are really

altered by accidentals, the change of Root is even more clearly apparent. For example, [musical notation] is the chord of the Dominant 7th on the Root G, resolving to the triad of C. If the note G in this chord is chromatically raised, thus: [musical notation], the chord is like the chord of the Diminished 7th built upon the Root E (which is of course omitted), resolving to the triad on A. Therefore, the Root of the chord, as well as the resolution, may be said to have been changed by the alteration of the single note. Consequently :

245. (5.) By a change of Root a change in the resolution is necessarily caused.

Now we will proceed to consider the Altered chords.

246. By reference to the foot-note, § 158, it becomes clear that the *natural* resolution of any dependent chord is to the triad a 4th higher than the Root of that Dependent chord; and we have just seen that when through a change of notation, or other causes, *the Root is changed*, the natural resolution of the chord is completely changed in consequence. This fact is illustrated in Fig. 68 and the accompanying text.

A change in a chord, whether of a note or simply in the notation, which produces a change of Root (and therefore of resolution), is called an *Harmonic* change. Where the change simply affects *one part transiently*, *not producing a change of Root and resolution*, the change is called a *Melodic* change.

Where a chromatic change in a note is made as suggested in § 238, the result must be one of two things:

either the Harmonic change just mentioned, or the Melodic change.

By an *Harmonic* change a completely new chord is formed, which is outside the key, speaking strictly, since it contains a note foreign to the scale of the key. Such changes will be considered under the head of Foreign Chords, Chapter XII.

By a *Melodic* change the alteration has more to do with a single part, rather than effecting any change in the character of the chord. Such changes produce Altered chords, if they have sufficient duration to be considered as chords; or Passing-notes, if of insufficient duration. Such alterations may occur in Chords of the 7th as well as in triads.

But the pupil will desire to distinguish between Altered chords and Foreign chords, and to discover the Roots and resolutions of the Foreign chords. The following is the method :—

To Distinguish between Altered Chords and Foreign Fundamental Chords.

247.   (1.) For convenient survey, place all the notes within the compass of one octave, striking out all duplicates.

(2.)   Place the chord in 3rds.   (See § 172.)

(3.)   Construct a descriptive formula of the 3rds as shown in § 239, and compare it with the formula of a Fundamental chord there shown. If they correspond, the chord in question is a Fundamental chord. If not, it is clear that either it was not originally a fundamental chord, or that some interval has been altered. (If the Root of such a chord is unknown to the pupil, he must discover the altered note or notes by comparison with the formula before proceeding to find the root by the method

outlined in the following paragraph.)   But, before proceeding, let us illustrate the above.

248.   For example, to find whether

is a Fundamental* or an Altered chord : —

Placing all the notes within the compass of one octave,

gives : .   Inverting, to obtain the required

figuring, we have successively :

the last being the required form.

Describing the 3rds as required in § 239, we have
the formula
$$7 \Big\} \text{minor.}$$
$$5 \Big\} \text{minor.}$$
$$3 \Big\} \text{minor.}$$
$$1$$

---

* It should be noticed that the Dominant is the only Fundamental chord
of the Seventh which is to be found in any key. The Secondary Sevenths do
not correspond perfectly in their intervals with the intervals of the Fundamental.
(This accounts, in part, for the prominence given to the various forms of Dominant harmony.)

Chords which are not Fundamental chords *may* be Secondary chords.
Therefore, if the formula does not correspond with the formula for a Fundamental chord, we should compare it with the Secondary chord having the same
Root (provided that the given Root represents a Secondary chord) before
deciding that it is an Altered chord.

Comparing with the standard formula :—

Standard Formula		Formula of the Given Chord :
9 } major or minor	. . . . . minor	{ .7
7 } minor . . . . . . · . minor		{ 5
5 } minor . . . . ⌣ . . minor		{ 3
3 } major		{ 1
1		

we find it agrees with it in every particular, as far as it goes. It is therefore a Fundamental chord without its root, i. e., a chord of the diminished 7th.

Again, to learn whether the chord is a

Fundamental chord or not :— Proceeding as before gives

the formula :

7 } major.

5 } minor.

3 } major.

1

Comparing this with the standard formula, we find that the intervals of the given chord cannot be made to correspond with three *successive* intervals in the standard formula. Thus

Standard Formula :		Formula of Given Chord :	
9 } major or minor	.	major { 7	: corresponds.
7 } minor	. . .	minor { 5	: corresponds.
5 } minor	. . . . . .	major { 3	: does not cor-
3 } major		{ 1	respond.
1			

Therefore, even if the Root of the given chord were found, whatever note it might be, it could never form a Fundamental chord in connection with the notes as given. Comparison with the chords of the 7th upon the various degrees of the scale, by comparing the formulæ, shows that this chord might be the Chord of the 7th upon the 1st degree of the scale of B♭ major, resolving naturally to the triad upon the 4th degree; e. g.

Exercises.

State whether the following chords are Altered chords, or Fundamental chords, or whether they might be secondary chords in some key:—

To Discover the Root of any Fundamental Chord.

249. (1.) Write all the notes in the compass of one octave, striking out duplicates.*

(2.) Place the notes in 3rds, as shown in § 247.

(3.) If it is a triad (three notes), the Root will be the lowest tone. (This is merely the result of the definition of the Direct form of a chord. See § 125.) It will now be apparent whether the chord is (1) an ordinary Major or Minor triad; (2) an Altered triad; or (3) an incomplete form of a Fundamental Dependent chord.

---

* Sometimes a note is omitted in a Chord of the 7th, or 7th and 9th. The pupil should refer to § 248, and observe how the intervals in the Fundamental chord would occur if the Root were omitted; for without the Root a different order of intervals would result, which might lead the pupil to think a chord to be an Altered chord when in reality it is an incomplete form of a Fundamental chord.

N. B.   Remember that a Diminished triad may be considered as an incomplete form of a Chord of the 7th, and resolve accordingly.   (See § 179.)

250.   If it is a Chord of the Seventh (four notes), we must first be sure that it is a Fundamental and not an Altered chord.   How to accomplish this is shown in § 247.   If shown to be a Fundamental chord, either with or without the Root, we may proceed as follows :— Compare the notes as shown in § 29, to discover which note is relatively the " sharpest " and which the " flattest."

In comparing the notes, *the sharpest one will be the Leading-note.*   (The *flattest* note will be the 9th, if it is a Chord of the 9th, otherwise it will be the 7th.) The Leading-note being a Major 3rd above the Root of a Fundamental Dependent chord, to find the Root when the Leading-note is known simply count a Major 3rd downward from that Leading-note.   (N. B.   The Root may not be present in the chord.   It never is in chords of the Diminished 7th.)   When the Root is found, it can be proven by the " flattest " notes, which should be the 9th or the 7th from the Root as above shown.   (For further explanation of this point, see " How to Modulate," p. 18.)

251.   *Illustration of preceding Section.*   To find the Root of .   Comparing the notes to find the " sharpest " note, we see that B is represented by five sharps; D by two sharps; F by one flat; and A♭ by four flats; consequently B is the " sharpest " note, and therefore the Leading-note.   As the Root of the chord should be a Major 3rd below the Leading-note, by counting downward a Major 3rd from B we find that G is the Root

of the chord. Building a Fundamental chord upon the Root G, we have G–B–D–F–A♭, which is a chord of the Minor 9th, and corresponds to the notes of the given chord. Therefore, the chord in question is a Chord of the Diminished 7th upon the Root G, resolving to the minor or major triad on C. (See §213.)

Again, to find the Root of the chord [music].

Comparing as before, we find that C♮ is represented by seven flats; D by two sharps; F by one flat; and A♭ by four flats; consequently, D is the " sharpest " note. A Major 3rd below D is B♭, which is consequently the Root of the chord. Placing the chord in 3rds, and writing the Root in its place, the full chord is seen to be a Chord of the Minor 9th upon the Root B♭.

252. *To discover in what key such a foreign chord is written*, simply remember that the " sharpest " note is the Leading-note, or 7th degree of the scale. There-fore, the chord [music] may be said to be written in the key of C minor, and the chord [music] in the key of E♭ minor. (See also " How to Modulate " § 20.)

Exercises.

253. Name the Roots and Keys of the following chords :—

Ambiguous Chords.

254. Sometimes a chord may occur which might be either an' Altered chord or a Foreign chord. E. g.,

F♯-C-D♯ might be either a chord derived from the Secondary 7th on the 2nd degree of C Major (by raising F
and D by accidentals;— notice that the chord appears
without the 5th;—write it), or it might be considered as
derived from a new Root, B, being an incomplete form of
the Chord of the Diminished 7th (write it).

To learn which of two Roots is intended, *examine
the resolution:* for if the resolution is the same as it
would have been without the alteration, it proves that
the chord is Altered; whereas, if the resolution is different, it shows that the chord is a Foreign chord. For
example, in the above, if the Altered chord derived
from the Root D is intended, the progression would
be to the chord G–C–E, which is considered as interpolated* between the chord on D and its natural resolution which follows. (See *a*, Fig. 73.) If the Root
B is intended, the resolution would be to the minor triad
on E (a 4th higher than B). (See *b*, Fig. 73.)

Fig. 73.

---

* By an interpolated chord is meant a chord placed between two chords
which naturally belong together. For example, the natural resolution of the
seventh-chord upon D is to the triad on G. But the chromatic alteration of the
note D, thus : ▒▒, inclines it away from its place in the chord of
G, and would cause an awkward effect should it return after starting else-
where. Consequently, the triad on C is interpolated for smoother effect; *but
the true resolution is only delayed,* for it enters immediately after. (See
Fig. 73, *a.*)

Treatment of Altered Chords.

255. As mentioned, any note of a chord may be altered by an accidental; and when the resulting change does not cause a change of Root, it is called simply an Altered chord; e. g., is the common triad on C; if the note G is raised chromatically, thus: we say that the note G has been altered from its original condition, and the whole triad might be called an altered triad. The triad has not been essentially changed (we still look upon C as the root), but the note G, having been raised, is strongly inclined to progress to the next note above, A. Such alterations may occur in seventh-chords as well as in triads.

256. The pupil needs little guidance in the treatment of Altered chords, other than to remember that the tendency of a chromatically raised note is to ascend, and the tendency of a chromatically lowered note is to descend. The general rule that accidental sharps tend upward, and accidental flats downward, is good to remember, but it does not convey the whole idea, for a *natural* may have the effect of *raising* a note previously flatted by signature or accidental; e. g., . The natural here raises the E♭ chromatically, and is similar to: . In the same way, a natural may chromatically lower a note: e. g., . Thus it is clear that flats, naturals and sharps are *relative* rather than *specific* terms.

A chromatically altered note, *being a tendency-note, should not be doubled.*

Altered Chords in General Use.

257.   Of the many altered chords, those most in use are ·

(*a.*)   The Triad with raised 5th;
(*b.*)   The Chord of the 7th with raised 5th;
(*c.*)   The Chords of the Augmented 6th;
(*d.*)   The Neapolitan 6th.   (See § 259.)

The progression of these *chords* is usually the same as if the unaltered intervals were present; while the progression of the altered notes depends upon the tendency of the accidental alteration.   The changes are simply melodic changes of a single part, for the purpose of variety or of softening a harsh effect.

Exercises.

(*a.*)   Write examples of all the above-mentioned Altered chords in various keys.

258. (*b.*)   Exercises.

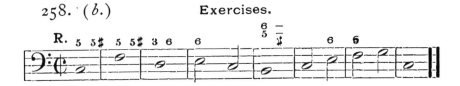

Advanced Course.

Neapolitan Sixth.

259.　(*Usual explanation.　For author's exposition of the chord, see* § 261.)

Among the altered chords is one in such common use as to receive a distinctive name.　When the triad on the 2nd degree of the Minor scale: with its Root lowered by an accidental

is used in its first inversion, a very soft effect is produced.　The chord is considered effective only in this inversion, and is called the Neapolitan Sixth; e. g.,

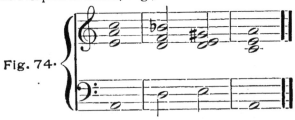

Fig. 74.

This alteration of the note on the 2nd degree is purely arbitrary, like the lowering of the 5th in the Chord of the Augmented 6th; and it is frequently used, probably on account of the fact that the natural (un-altered) triad on the 2nd degree in Minor is a Diminished triad, and therefore has tendencies of too pronounced character for effective use in ordinary chord-connections (not resolutions). It was found, however, that by lowering this note the apparent tendency was hidden, making the chord more manageable.

Exercises.

260. Form chords of the Neapolitan 6th from the triad on the 2nd degree of every Minor key, and resolve them.

Derivation of the Neapolitan Sixth-Chord.

261. (*The following is submitted entirely upon the author's responsibility.*)

The Neapolitan Sixth is believed to be a *form of the Augmented sixth-chord, with sufficient license in its treatment* to admit of the smoothest effect in Minor.

The following examples will illustrate the assertion and the grounds for the belief.

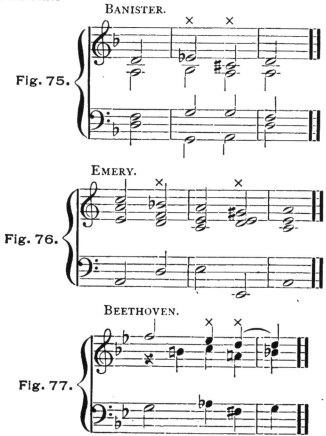

BANISTER.

Fig. 75.

EMERY.

Fig. 76.

BEETHOVEN.

Fig. 77.

The license mentioned above is this :— That the notes comprising the full chord of the Augmented 6th *are often divided between two chords.* The chords marked ✕ in the illustrations are the chords in question.

If the chord marked ✕ in Fig. 75 is a chord of the Augmented 6th, it is the 5th from the Root which is altered by an accidental. The altered note being E♭, the root should be A. Let us assume that the Root *is* A, and develop the chord from it. The chord of the Minor 9th upon A, (from which the Chord of the Augmented 6th is devel-

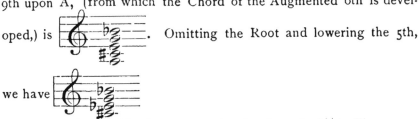

oped,) is [music]. Omitting the Root and lowering the 5th,

we have [music]

Now, this chord is the same as the chord marked ✕ in Fig. 75, excepting that the Leading-note, C♯, *which appears in the next chord*, is absent, leading us to think that the notes have been divided between the two chords.

262. Again, in § 224, the chord of the Augmented 6th is shown in Major, with the dominant of the key as the Root. Notice that, when the Dominant is the Root, *it is the 2nd degree of the scale which is the chromatically altered note.* If the above assertion is wrong, is it not rather strange that the note which is altered by an accidental to produce the chord of the Augmented 6th in Major should happen to be the same note that is so altered in the Minor key? And is it not still more strange that the resolution of the two chords should be the same? And is it not strange that the process of building a Fundamental chord upon the chosen Root should result in the desired Chord of the Neapolitan Sixth?

In further proof, the example in Fig. 76 is offered. Here the Neapolitan 6th, marked ✕, which is built upon the Root E (since the chromatically altered 5th above the root is B♭), resolves directly to the triad on A (a 4th higher than E) without the help of any other chord. Notice, however, that the next chord comes in to supply the Leading-note, for the cadence has not been quite strong enough without it.

The next example, Fig. 77, from Beethoven, refutes the idea that the chord is good in only one inversion. Here the chords marked ✕ have the chord of the Augmented 6th divided between them, and the notes, though identical with those of the other examples, are in a different inversion, giving an excellent effect.

It is submitted that the example from Beethoven is as effective as the examples in Fig. 75 and 76.

The pupil is recommended to read §§ 42–50 in "How to Modulate."

Exercises.

263. Form chords of the Neapolitan 6th, from the Dominant as a Root, in every Minor key, and resolve them.

264. Attention is again called to the wonderful simplicity of the system of developing the chords shown in this volume. By bringing the chords of the Dominant 7th, Minor and Major 9th, Diminished 7th, Augmented $\frac{6}{3}$, Augmented $\frac{6}{4}$, and Augmented $\frac{6}{5}$, and the Neapolitan 6th all under one head, derived from the same Root, having the same dissonant intervals, and the same natural resolution, one is inclined to accept the statement that " There is but one chord in the Universe, the Common Chord. All others are merely additions to this chord."

Synopsis.

Write the usual synopsis of the chapter.

CHAPTER XII.

FOREIGN CHORDS.

265. The object of this chapter is to enable the student to recognize some of those chords which, though technically foreign to the key, so constantly intermingle with chords which belong wholly to the key. These foreign chords have such a peculiarly close relationship to the chords of the key, that we cannot well say that we are in a foreign key when they occur, but that a foreign key is suggested or touched. (See Grove's Dictionary of Music, Vol. II, p. 351.)

The following chapter will be developed from a principle which is already familiar to the pupil, viz.,

The Natural Resolution of Dominant Harmony to the Tonic.

266. By Dominant harmony is not meant the chord
of the Dominant 7th alone, but also the chord of the Dominant 9th (both Major and Minor), the Chord of the
Diminished 7th, and the various forms of the Augmented
Sixth-chord, which are all forms of Dominant harmony,
and resolve to the Tonic.

Exercises.

Preliminary to the following, and to enable the
pupil easily to grasp the subject, he should *form chords
like the Dominant 7th, upon every (chromatic) degree
of the scale, and resolve them, like the Dominant 7th,
to the triad a 4th higher.* Do not write any signatures,
and do not call them Dominant and Tonic chords. Simply notice that the Chord of the 7th upon any note resolves to the triad a 4th higher, and observe that the tendency of the seventh-chord toward the triad a 4th higher
is so strong that there is clearly a close relationship between the two chords. This relationship is the same as
the relationship of Dominant to Tonic, but they *should
not be called* Dominant and Tonic unless they are considered as belonging to some key, and that is not now
desired. The object here is *to show the relationship of
the two chords*, whether they are in a key or are considered by themselves.

The intervals of a chord of the Dominant 7th are a
Major 3rd, a Perfect 5th, and a Minor 7th. Therefore,
in forming these chords, the pupil will see that these
intervals are present, and will use accidental sharps and

flats to secure them. (These chords are the same as the Fundamental chords described in the last chapter.)

267. The next step is to learn the reverse of the above, viz.,— To find that chord of the 7th which shall resolve to any given triad, Major or Minor.

Process.

As a chord of the 7th resolves naturally to the triad a 4th higher, to find the triad which shall resolve to a given triad, we simply need to look a 4th lower than the Root of the triad.

Illustration. To find the chord of the 7th which shall resolve to the triad (Major or Minor) upon A :— Looking a Perfect 4th below A, we find E to be the Root of the desired chord of the 7th. Completing the chord of the 7th upon E, by the addition of a Major 3rd, Perfect 5th and Minor 7th, we find the full chord to be ·

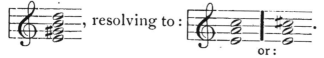

, resolving to :   .
                                        or :

N. B. Remember that the chord of the 7th resolves to either Major or Minor, since the chord of the Dominant 7th of A Major is the same as in A Minor.

Exercises.

268. Taking each (chromatic) degree of the scale, in turn, find the Chord of the 7th which will resolve to the triad upon that degree. Complete the chord of the 7th, and resolve it to the proper triad, as above shown.

269. The pupil has now learned, that there is a Chord of the 7th *closely related to every Major and Minor triad.* Therefore it would not be strange to find, that these related chords are sometimes used, although they are not, strictly speaking, in the key.

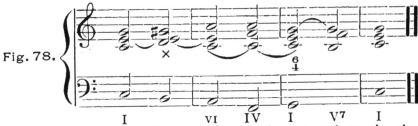

Fig. 78.

I   VI   IV   I   V7   I

Notice that the chord marked × is not strictly in the key of C, but is apparently like the Dominant 7th in the key of A. It does lead to the *chord* of A, and is in so far like the chord of the Dominant 7th in the key of A. But the chord on A is in the key of C (on the 6th degree). Now let it be noticed that the chord marked × is *like* the chord of the Dominant 7th : but *as there can be but one chord of the Dominant 7th in a key*, we must adopt some other way of describing the relation of this chord to the triad on A, and will call it the *"Attendant"* chord of A. (The reason for thus naming such chords is more clearly described in the author's " How to Modulate.")

270.   From a consideration of the above, §§ 265 to 269, it is clear that each major and minor triad in any key has its attendant chord.* As shown in the following example, these attendant chords can be used with good effect. They are indicated by [A].

Fig. 79.

I   [A]   II   [A]   V   [A]

---

* The triads upon the 7th degree in Major, and the 2nd and 7th in Minor, are prohibited from having [A] chords The reason for this prohibition is, that being Diminished triads, and therefore not consonant, they could not be the resolution of a dissonance (see § 151), and therefore could not stand in the relation of Tonic, which would be required if they were to have [A] chords. (It has been shown that although not Tonic and Dominant, a triad and its [A] chord stand *in the relationship* of Tonic and Dominant.)   For the same reason, the Augmented triads in Minor are prohibited from having [A] chords.

VI   [A]   III   [A]   IV   [A]   V   V⁷   I

N. B. In practical composition, [A] chords would not be so frequently used as in the above exámple, which is given to show how the [A] chord of every Major and Minor triad in the key can be used.

Exercises.

271. (*a.*) Taking the key of G, find in succession the [A] chords which shall resolve to the triads o꜀ II, III, IV, V, and VI, proceeding as in § 267.

(*b.*) In a similar way, take all the Major and Minor keys in turn.

Much repetition and persevering practice are necessary to give the required proficiency. Before proceeding, the pupil must be able to give instantly the [A] chord of any Major or Minor triad.

272. It is remarkable what frequent use of the [A] chords has. been made by composers, beginning with Beethoven. In the following example, from Mendelssohn's Spring Song, are five [A] chords in seven measures. The explanation is found in the marking under the staff. For example, [A] of II means the [A] chord resolving to the triad on the second degree of the scale. Therefore, after the [A] of II we may expect to hear the chord on II. In the second measure we do hear it, but as it has a major 3rd D♯, it becomes also the [A] of V.

For further explanation of this example see " How to Modulate," p. 7.

Fig. 80.

273. The pupil should examine some of Beethoven's Sonatas, and also examples from Mendelssohn, finding the [A] chords and indicating by proper marking to which degree of the scale they are attendant. He should also be on the alert to find examples of [A] chords in the music in daily use.

Exercises.

274. Write little successions of chords introducing one or two [A] chords. Be careful not to wander away from the key, but see that each [A] chord resolves to some triad in the key. There need be but three or four chords, after which a close may be reached by a Closing cadence.

275. A remarkable feature of [A] chords is that they give great variety by enlarging the boundaries of the key, so to speak, instead of confining everything to the chords upon the seven degrees of the scale, and their inversions.

Another highly practical use of the [A] chords is their wonderful power in modulating. This will be explained in the following chapter.

Synopsis.

Form as usual.

CHAPTER XIII.

MODULATION.

276. *Modulation* is the passing from one key to another; and is effected by the use of one or more chords characteristic of (belonging to) the key *to which* it is desired to modulate.

There are innumerable ways of modulating, but the very multiplicity of the means employed has always made it most difficult for the beginner to grasp them, and the usual result is utter confusion of ideas, and little practical skill in passing from key to key. The method here presented is held to be simple, systematic, and comprehensive.

277. Modulation is effected by connecting some chord of the " old key " with some chord in the " new key." (N. B." Old key " and " new key " refer, respectively, to the key *from* which, and the key *to* which, it is desired to modulate.) Therefore, if we can find a method of connecting *any* two triads, the difficulty is easily solved.

Notice, we do not say that Modulation is effected by connecting the " old " Tonic triad with the " new " Tonic triad; but by connecting *any* (Major or Minor) triad of the " old " key with any of the " new " key. Our range of possibilities in variety and delicacy, and means of hiding the modulation, is therefore very large if we can master this one point, viz., *to connect any two triads.*

To Connect any Two Triads.

278.   It has been shown at the beginning of study how chords are connected by means of a common note.   (See § 102.)   We have also studied in the last chapter the system of Attendant chords, and learned that any Major or Minor triad may have its appropriate [A] chord.

Upon trial it will be found that *if there is no direct connection between two given chords by means of a com mon note, the connection can be made by the use of one or both of their Attendant Chords.*   Thus it becomes possible to connect *any* two chords without considering whether they belong to the same key or to different keys.

For example, let us connect the chord of C with the chord of F♯.   As there is no common note to connect the two triads, we will write them with their Attendant chords, which we will indicate by [A].

The second chord in Fig. 81 is the [A] chord of C, the third chord that of F♯.

Fig. 81.

[A] of *C*. [A] of *F♯*.

279. Usually only one [A] chord is necessary, as for example in connecting the triads of C and D Major, shown in Fig. 82.

Fig. 82.

[A] of *D*.

Thus it will be seen that although two chords may not have a common note to connect them, when we consider their Attendant chords a connecting-link will become apparent.

280.   In the following exercises the pupil will connect two given Major or Minor triads.*   The mental process, given below, will be of much assistance.   The example given to illustrate the process is :—To connect the triad of C major with the triad of B♭ major.—

Process.

Given, *to connect the triad of C with the triad of B♭* :—

1st Step.   What are the [A] chords of the triad *from* which and the triad *to* which we would pass?**

Ans.   The [A] of the triad on C is G–B–D–F

The [A] of the triad on B♭ is F–A–C–E♭.

(Write the notes for reference).

---

* Should any two triads have a common note, the connection may be made without the help of the [A] chords.   But in many cases it will be observed that the use of the [A] chords gives a smoother connection and more repose when the final chord is reached.

** For the present we will use the [A] chords in the form of a chord of the 7th.

2nd Step. Is there any note common to the triad of C and the [A] of B♭.

Ans. Yes, C is common to the two chords, and will enable us to make the connection.

3rd Step. Of the four chords before us, viz., the triad on C and its [A]; and the triad on B♭ and its [A]; how many do we need to make a good connection?

Ans. Three, the triad on C, the [A] of B♭ and the triad on B♭.

4th Step. Write them, trying to secure a good leading of the parts.

Fig. 83.

Could this connection be made in any other way?

Ans. Yes, both [A] chords could be used instead of one, as there is a note common to both [A] chords. F is that common note.

The connection using both [A] chords is shown in Fig. 84.

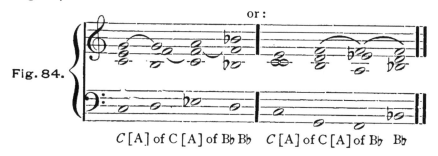

Fig. 84.

Exercises.

N. B. While working out these exercises, the pupil should constantly refer to the notes in §§ 282–284.

281. (*a.*) Connect the major triad on C with the major triad on C♯.

Connect the major triad on C with the major triad on D.

Connect the major triad on C with the major triad on D♯.

Connect the major triad on C with the major triad on E.

And so on, till the triad on C has been connected with every other triad. Then—

(*b.*) Connect the triad on C♯ with the major triad on C.

Connect the triad on C♯ with the major triad on D.

Connect the triad on C♯ with the major triad on D♯.

And continue through the chromatic scale as before.

(*c.*) Starting from the triad upon each remaining note of the scale, connect with every other triad.

(*d.*) Connect as above each Minor triad with all other Minor triads; and with all Major triads.

282. In doing the above exercises, it may be possible to make many connections in two or more ways, viz.,

(*a.*) Without any [A] chord.

(*b.*) Using the [A] chord of the triad *to* which we pass.

(*c.*) Using the [A] chord of the triad *from* which we pass.

(*d.*) Using both [A] chords.

N. B. The Enharmonic change is often employed, changing sharps to flats, and vice versa.

283. If only one [A] chord is used, that of the triad *to* which we progress will usually be the better one, for the following reason:

The natural tendency of an [A] chord is strongly

toward *its* triad, like the tendency of a Dominant seventh-chord towards its Tonic triad.   Therefore, in connecting two triads, if the [A] of the one *from* which we go is used, the natural tendency would be to *return* to that triad; whereas, if the [A.] of the triad *to* which we go is used, there is a natural tendency to continue to that desired triad.   This explains why some of the connections made by the pupil will be harsh and forced.   (The next paragraph will show how the above-mentioned tendency to return may be hidden, and the harshness avoided.)   The difference in effect between the [A] *from* which, and the [A] *to* which we go, is illustrated in Fig. 85.

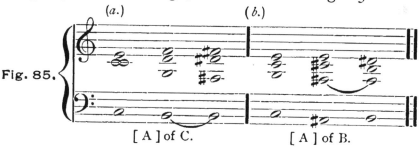

Fig. 85.

[A] of C.   [A] of B.

(*a*) is not positively bad in effect; but the superiority of (*b*), using the [A] of the triad to which we pass, is manifest in its smoothness and repose.

284.   *To remove the Tendency to return shown in the* [A] *of the triad from which we progress.*—It will be found that by *inverting* this [A] chord, the natural tendency toward its triad is to a great extent hidden.   In composition, chords are inverted not only to give variety, but also to induce a smoother leading of the individual parts.   *Thus the melodic tendencies of individual parts become more prominent, and the harmonic tendencies less so.*

From this we learn that :—

(*a.*)   Inverting an [A] chord reduces the force of its characteristic tendency toward its triad.

(*b.*)   Melodic tendencies of the individual parts also serve to cover the same tendency.

This is illustrated in Fig. 86, where the same connection as in (*a*), Fig. 85, is given, using the [A] of the triad from which we pass, and producing a very satisfactory effect.

Fig. 86.

[A] of C.

Therefore:—In using the [A] 'of the triad *from* which you progress, always invert it, and consider the melodic tendencies, making the individual parts progress with as little skipping as possible.

To Connect any Two Keys.

285.   Having learned to connect any two triads, we proceed to connect any two keys; for it is evident, that the connection (or modulation) is effected by selecting a triad from the old key and one from the new key, and finding the connection *between these two triads*, as shown above.   And when the two triads are connected, the keys are thereby connected, and the modulation is effected. Therefore, the connections shown in Figures 81 to 86, might be taken as a method of passing from one *key* to another, instead of from one *chord* to another.

Exercises.

286.   (*a.*)   From every Major key modulate to every other Major and every Minor key.

(*b.*)   From every Minor key modulate to every other Minor key and every Major key.

287. Note I. It should be observed that the [A] chords resolve equally well to Major and Minor triads. Therefore, the Major and Minor triad of any degree (for example, the Major triad of G and the Minor triad of G) would both have the same [A] chord.

288. Note II. Notice that the [A] of the Tonic chord (or key) to which we modulate is nothing more or less than the chord of the Dominant Seventh resolving to its Tonic.

289. Note III. To thoroughly establish the new tonality (or consciousness of the new key), the Closing Formula should follow the connection of the two triads, particularly if the triad to which we progress appears in an inversion. The sense of incompleteness without the Closing Formula is illustrated in the following :

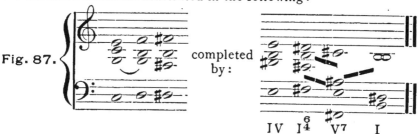

Fig. 87.

completed by :

IV I$_4^6$ V^7 I

290. In the preceding pages, we have learned to con nect any two triads, and, in a similar way, any two keys. The process, being founded upon a principle *which is followed implicitly in all cases*, might be represented by a formula which shall give a visible plan of procedure, and show between which chords the [A] chords are to be introduced, if at all. The chord-connections shown in §§ 278 to 288, would be represented by the formula :—

Old Chord,　　[A],　　New Chord.

The method of connecting two keys by connecting the tonic triad of the old key with the tonic triad of the new key would be :—

$$\frac{I}{\text{Old Key}}, \qquad [A], \qquad \frac{I}{\text{New Key}},$$

291. The terms Old key, and New key, are used to indicate briefly that the chords designated by the Roman

Numerals belong to the key *from* which, or the key *to* which, we modulate.

The Roman Numerals indicate upon which degree of the scale the chord (a common triad when not otherwise indicated) is to be taken.

[A] indicates that an Attendant chord is to be inserted if necessary. Sometimes two [A] chords may be employed to advantage.

292. Observe that the [A] of $\dfrac{\text{I}}{\text{New Key}}$ is simply the chord of the Dominant Seventh in the new key. As the progression of an [A] to its triad is precisely the same as that of a Chord of the Dominant Seventh to its Tonic triad, we may draw the logical conclusion that *if we can pass to the Tonic of a Foreign key through its Dominant chord, we can pass to any other Major or Minor triad of a foreign key by using Attendant chords.*

As these Attendant chords are so easily found, and have a most intimate relation with their Primary chords, they will prove a simple, practical and correct means of connecting the original key with *any desired chord* of the new key.

293. With the assistance of the Attendant chords it becomes possible to formulate the principal methods of Modulation, giving a most thorough and comprehensive view of the whole subject.

If we modulate by means of the Dominant Seventh-chord of the new key, we must connect the original key and the *New Dominant ;* if we modulate through some other chord of the new key, *we must connect with that chord.* Upon this plan the Formulæ are constructed.

Modulation by Means of the Dominant Seventh-Chord of the New Key.

294. According to the heading of this section, we must pass through $\underset{\text{New key}}{\underline{\quad V^7 \quad}}$; therefore, the first problem is to connect $\underset{\text{Old key}}{\underline{\quad I \quad}}$ and $\underset{\text{New key}}{\underline{\quad V^7 \quad}}$. Should there be a note common to both chords, we can proceed at once to the desired chord. If not, the *Principle of Attendant Chords* will supply the connection. Thus, the formula becomes $\underset{\text{Old key}}{\underline{\quad I \quad}}$, [A] $\underset{\text{New key}}{\underline{\quad V^7,^* \; I \quad}}$. Observe that [A] may indicate the [A] chord of *either* the Old Tonic or the New Dominant, or of *both* if necessary.

To illustrate, let us modulate from C to F♯.

Now the formula becomes more specific: $\underset{\text{Old key}}{\underline{\qquad I \qquad}}$ represents the triad on C: $\underset{\text{New key}}{\underline{\qquad I \qquad}}$ represents that on F♯, and $\underset{\text{New key}}{\underline{\qquad V^7 \qquad}}$ the Dominant Seventh-chord on C♯. As there is no connecting-note between the chord on C and that on C♯, we resort to the Attendant Chords, and discover that we can use *either* the Attendant chord of C or that of C♯.

Writing the chords and the formula together shows plainly the connection, using first the [A] chord of $\underset{\text{Old key}}{\underline{\quad I \quad}}$ and then the [A] chord of $\underset{\text{New key}}{\underline{\quad V \quad}}$, as represented in Figs. 88 and 89.

---

*An [A] chord can resolve to a Seventh-chord instead of to a simple triad, on the ground that one Dominant Seventh-chord can resolve to another (See § 185.)

Fig. 88.

I, [A] of I   V⁷,   I

Old key   New key

Fig. 89.

I   [A] of V, V⁷,   I.

Old key   New key

295. In every case of Modulation through the Dominant Seventh of the new key, there will be a feeling of incompleteness. This will disappear if, after the new Tonic has been reached, the "Closing Formula" is added. This is illustrated in Fig. 90, where the same Modulation as in Fig. 89 is given, with a slightly different leading of the parts on account of the Closing Formula following.

Fig. 90.

I, [A] of V, V⁷,   I   II   I⁶₄,   V⁷   I.

Old key   New key   Closing Formula

Exercises.

296. For the first exercises, start from the Tonic triad of C and pass to all other keys *through the new Domi-*

nant Seventh-chord, using the [A] chords if necessary to make the connection. Next, proceed from C♯ to every other key; then from D; and so on, till *every key has been used as a starting-point* from which to modulate to *every other key.* To gain the fullest benefit, the pupil should practise modulating *both at the keyboard and in writing:*

297. Attention must be paid to the *correct leading of the parts.* A Modulation which is harsh in one position and with a certain leading of the parts, may often be much improved and softened by a change of position and different movement of the parts.

It will be found that while many of these Modulations are harsh in spite of a good leading of the parts, when made *directly* through the new Dominant Seventh *they may be made very pleasant by the use of one or both* [A]*chords.* The student must not fear to take the chords in their different inversions to induce a smooth leading of the parts.

A good effect depends also upon a proper arrangement of the accents, as shown in § 190. (See also "How to Modulate," § 15.)

298. When we use the [A] chord of the new Dominant, we touch the *key* of the Dominant of the new key, as we make use of the Seventh-chord on its (the Dominant's) Fifth degree. Thus, in Fig. 89, the new key is F♯ and the key of its Dominant is C♯. Now it will be seen that the [A] chord, having B♯, is like the Dominant Seventh-chord in the *key* of C♯. Dr. Stainer says, in his "Composition," that a new key should be entered through *related chords or related keys.* Here it is plain that we have entered through a related key,— that of the Dominant. Thus it appears how the *System of Attendant Chords* fills the requirements of related chords or related keys in Modulation.

Change of Mode.

299. The change from a Major key to the Minor key of like name (e. g., C Major to C Minor) cannot be

called a modulation, since the key-note is not changed, but merely the mode. Notice that the chord of the Dominant 7th is the same in both Major and Minor, and that the two triads may follow each other without the interposition of any modulating chord (Fig. 91, *a*) ; or the common Dominant 7th may be interposed (Fig. 91, *b*). Many examples of this interchange between Major and Minor may be found in the works of the masters.

Fig. 91.

300. In the preceding paragraphs we have entered the new key at the Tonic triad or the Chord of the Dominant. It is equally convenient to enter at *any other* (Major or Minor) *triad* of the scale. To construct the formula for such a case, we should merely substitute the desired degree for the term $\dfrac{\text{V}}{\text{New key}}$.

It is also possible to leave the " old " key at points other than the Tonic triad.

The [A] chords can be used, not only in the form of seventh-chords, but also in the form of Diminished 7ths, Augmented 6ths, or Chords of the 9th. These different methods, together with the possible different points of leaving the old and entering the new key, offer great variety in the means of modulation. The chord of the Diminished seventh is especially useful in Modulation, since it has a direct and natural resolution to *four different* chords. (See § 215.) Having just seen that it is possible to enter the new key at various points, each one of the above-mentioned chords of resolution might be considered either the Tonic, Dominant or Supertonic of a key.* In this way, each one of the four chords might represent not *one*, but *three* different keys. The four different chords would then together represent twelve different keys; i. e., *all* the different keys. It is therefore possible to modulate from *any* chord of the Diminished seventh *directly into any one of the twelve Major and twelve Minor keys.*

By means of the above-mentioned methods, it is possible to pass directly from any key to any other. This is a most desirable accomplishment for organists, concert-players and accompanists, who are frequently called upon to bring two wholly unrelated keys into immediate proximity in successive selections. But it must be understood that such promiscuous intermingling of keys is never allowed in constructing any single piece of music. In Composition the range of selection is usually limited to the "Related keys;" viz., the keys of the Dominant, Subdominant, and their Relative Minors, and the Relative Minor of the key itself. (See §§ 39 and 334.)

Modulation by Means of a Common Triad.

In connecting two related keys, it will be found that instead of a single common note serving as a connecting-link, there is a complete chord which is common to both keys, offering the closest possible connection. E. g., in connecting the keys of C and G, the following triads will be found the same in both keys:—C: I and G: IV; C: III and G: VI; C: VI and G: II. Any one of these chords may be used as the connecting-link, the chord being approached as belonging to the key of C and left

---

* Each of these chords could just as well be taken as a Mediant, Subdominant or Submediant, as for Supertonic or Dominant. The three selected are merely more prominent, and suffice to enable one to modulate to *all* keys.

as belonging to the key of **G,** as shown in the marking under the illustration.

Exercises.

Starting from various keys in turn, modulate, by means of a common triad, to each of the related keys, as mentioned above.

There are also many other ways of modulating, which are not so comprehensive in their application as those already described, but are useful where circumstances happen to favor their introduction. Being of good effect and in common use, a few of them are mentioned:—(*a*) Compound modulation, passing through a series of keys to the one desired: (*b*) Single Note Connection; (*c*) By means of the False Cadence; (*d*) By means of Enharmonic Change.

All the above-named means of modulation, together with the principles of artistic modulation, are described in detail in the author's " How to Modulate."

Synopsis.

Write as usual.

PART III.

CHAPTER XIV.

VARIETY OF STRUCTURE : SUSPENSIONS : ANTICIPATIONS : RETARDATIONS.

301. For the purpose of giving variety to the harmonic structure of a composition, many devices are employed. Among them may be mentioned *Suspensions, Anticipations, Retardations, Passing-Notes, Passing-Chords, Changing-Notes, Appoggiaturas, Organ-Points, Sustained Notes, and Syncopations.*

These devices should not be looked upon as altering the principles of chord-construction already learned, but as means of giving greater variety to a composition. They are to Musical Composition what interior decoration is to Architecture, merely a means of ornamenting and enriching a substantial structure.

Suspensions.

302. In a succession of chords, when one tone is delayed, or held over till after the next chord has entered, a dissonance is formed, called a Suspension. This delayed and therefore dissonant tone moves but one step down or up, usually down, to its tone of resolution in the next chord.

The essential features of a suspension are :— the *Preparation*, the *Dissonance*, and the *Resolution*. The Preparation consists in the suspended tone being previously heard as an essential part of a chord. The Dissonance, technically called the Percussion, is caused by the progression of a single part being delayed while the remaining parts proceed. The Resolution is effected by allowing the delayed tone to proceed to its place in the following chord. In Fig. 92, the Suspension is in the Alto; the first note is the preparation; the second, connected with the first by a tie, is the Dissonance, or Percussion; and the third note the note of Resolution.

Fig. 92.

303. Let the pupil notice the following conditions implied by the definition and illustrated in Fig. 92 :—

(*a.*) One note is held over and prevented from progressing with the others. This is accomplished by the use of the tie.

(*b.*) By being heard in the first chord, the suspended tone is prepared. The Preparation should be as long as the Dissonance, else the Preparation would not be sufficiently marked.

(*c.*) The Preparation, Dissonance, and Resolution should be in the same part. Otherwise we could not have (particularly in vocal music) any effect of Preparation or of Resolution.

(*d.*) The Suspension, or rather the Dissonance,

should be heard on an accented part of the measure. A Dissonance on an unaccented part of a measure is not so prominent, and might be considered as a passing effect, i. e., a passing-note. But as the peculiar effect of suspense is desired, it is necessary to bring it into the foreground by placing it upon a prominent (accented) beat.

(*e.*) The tone that is delayed should not be heard meanwhile in another part, else there could not be the effect of suspense or delay. An exception to this is when the Bass takes the note of resolution at a distance of not less than an octave from the suspended tone, when it will not be disturbing.

(*f.*) The purity of the part-writing must not be forgotten. Suspensions do not excuse consecutive 5ths or 8ves, though one part may be delayed.*

(*g.*) A Dissonance is presupposed in a Suspension. Therefore, in passages where the delayed tone does not create a dissonance, there is not technically a Suspension, though it is treated precisely as if it were.

(*h.*) The suspended tone should move but one step to its tone of resolution. Where the delayed tone progresses by a skip, it is classed among Retardations. (See § 312.)

Figuring Suspensions.

304. Like other chords, Suspensions are figured by counting from the Bass note. To completely express a suspension by figures, requires that both the dissonance and the resolution be figured.

Exercises.

305. (*a.*) Turning back to the exercises in the early

---

* It is held by some writers that a Suspension *does* cover bad progressions or consecutives, which are therefore allowed where the effect is good.

pages of the book, the pupil may try to introduce Suspensions into the chord-connections, trying the various positions and deciding which are practical.   It will be found that all are not equally effective.

(*b.*)   Write examples of simple chord-connections and try to introduce Suspensions into all the different parts. Write in various keys.

306.   Exercises.

307. Suspensions may occur in two or more parts at once, in which case they are subject to the same rules as when occurring in only one part. (Fig. 93, *a.*)

Suspensions may also occur with a progressing Bass, i. e., while the tone of resolution is sounding, the Bass progresses to another tone, thus producing a new chord formation (Fig. 93, *b*), or another inversion of the same chord.

Fig. 93.

Suspensions may also be resolved ornamentally, i. e by the use of interpolated notes between the suspended note and its resolution. The note of resolution must be the same as if no ornaments were introduced (Fig. 93, *c*).

308. **Exercises.**

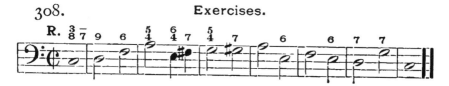

Open Position.

Anticipations.

309. ′ In a Suspension one tone of a chord is held over till after the next chord has entered. Anticipation is in one sense the reverse of this, for, instead of being delayed, a tone is *advanced*, or heard before the rest of the chord. Differently expressed, it is where a tone of one chord is anticipated in the previous chord. This is shown by the notes marked × in Fig. 94.

Fig. 94.

310. Notice the following in reference to the above example :

(*a.*) *Unimportant positions: Suspensions* occur upon the accented parts of a measure; *Anticipations*, upon unaccented parts. Anticipated notes are also usually short, never taking more than half the value of the preceding note, and usually less. Anticipations, therefore, are seen to occupy unimportant positions, in respect to both rhythm and duration.

(*b.*) Anticipations are usually restruck, i. e., not tied to the note which they anticipate.

(*c.*) Anticipations do not need to be prepared and resolved like Suspensions. They may enter freely by skips, and proceed by skips if desired.

Exercises.

311. Form examples of Anticipations in various keys.

Retardations.

312. Retardations are the opposite of Anticipations. A tone of the chord is held over while the remaining tones progress to the next chord. Retardations differ from Suspensions in being treated freely like Anticipations; i. e., they require no preparation, but may enter by skips; and (*b*) they are allowed to progress by skips, not being forced, like Suspensions, to progress to the note only one degree higher or lower.

Fig. 95.

Exercises.

313. (*a.*) Form examples of Retardations, in various keys.

(*b.*) Form examples, mingling Anticipations and Retardations.

Syncopation.

314. Syncopation is a kind of irregular Rhythm, where the more important notes are placed upon unimportant beats or parts of beats ; or where the notes fall between the beats. It may be produced by Anticipation or by Retardation ; i. e., by pushing forward one part ahead of the others, or by holding it back till the others have moved. Fig. 95 is an example, the note marked × serving to form a Syncopation, which is continued by the retarded notes marked o.

Synopsis.

Write as usual.

CHAPTER XV.

UNESSENTIAL NOTES: PASSING-NOTES.

315. Those notes which, coming after a chord, are not essential to it, but lie between the essential notes, are called Passing-notes.

Fig. 96.

Notice the following :—

(1.)   In Fig. 96 the notes marked × do not belong to the chords.

(2.)   These marked notes serve to connect the chord-notes melodically. with each other. In Fig. 96, (*b*), the chords are like those at (*a*), but in (*a*) the notes marked × serve to lead very smoothly from one chord to the next.

(3.)   These Passing-notes may occur in any part. They are usually found upon the unaccented portions of the measure, when they are called Regular Passing-notes; but are occasionally found upon the accented parts, when they are called Irregular Passing-notes.

(4.)   The harmonic structure of a composition is of the first importance, forming the basis or skeleton. The passing-notes and other ornaments are to be added afterward.

316.   Passing-notes may be chromatic as well as diatonic. In Fig. 97 the notes marked o are chromatic; those marked × are diatonic.

Fig. 97.

The pupil should find and write the chords forming the harmonic structure of Fig. 97, as shown at (*b*), Fig. 96.

Care must be exercised in securing a correct leading of the parts in the structure of the harmonies, i. e., in the chords before the passing-notes are added, since concealed 5ths and 8ves may, by the use of Passing-notes, become open consecutives.

Exercises.

317. Return to the first exercises, Chapters I and II, and insert passing-notes where possible, either in the given Bass or in the upper parts.

Exercises in Harmonizing the Scale.

Harmonize the scale, using Passing-notes where possible, together with the chords previously learned.

318. Two or more Passing-notes may be used simultaneously, or even all the notes in a chord, thus forming a Passing-chord. Occurring upon unaccented parts of a measure, Passing-chords are not expected to always harmonize perfectly, but may be looked upon rather as a number of Passing-notes leading melodically to the next chord upon an accented part of the measure; for upon the principal beats the harmony should be quite correct, though liberties are allowed on the weak beats.

Fig. 98.

319. The pupil may not clearly distinguish between altered chords and chords with chromatic passing-notes. The following constitutes the difference :—

(1.) To be an Altered chord, the tempo should be slow enough, and the accents such as to allow the altered note to be heard as part of a chord. A chromatic or diatonic scale-passage, accompanied by a single chord would be said to consist principally of passing-notes; e. g.,

Fig. 99.

(2.) Only chromatic alterations can be considered in connection with altered chords. If another note of the scale is substituted for a note of a chord (making a diatonic instead of a chromatic change), it is, of course, a passing-note. A note may be said to belong to a chord even if it has two flats or sharps before it, but as soon as it changes its name, it loses its membership in that particular chord; e. g., F× belongs to the triad:

but if we call it G, it could not belong to the triad of D♯.

Auxiliary Notes.

320. An Auxiliary note is one used for ornament or embellishment, and is found one degree above or below its principal note, which belongs to the chord. It precedes the principal note, and is heard either with or before the remaining notes of the chord; e. g.,

Fig. 100.

The peculiarity of the Auxiliary note is, that while it may enter by a skip (i. e., need not be prepared), it must progress by a single step to its note of resolution. (See Fig. 100.) These notes are also called Changing-notes, Appoggiaturas, and Free Suspensions.

321. Trills, Shakes, Turns and all similar ornaments are classed with Auxiliary notes. This principle is well expressed in " Musical Composition," Goetschius (N. Y. G. Schirmer), as follows : "Every harmonic interval is attended by four Neighboring tones, consisting in the next higher and lower Letters, in their notation as whole step and. half-step. Thus :

Exercises.

Fig. 101.

The Neighboring tone cannot be chromatic (as at Fig. 101, *b*), because the Letters must differ.

" The Neighboring tones may occur in almost any connection with their own harmonic interval (Principal tone) as Unessential or Embellishing notes.

" All the common forms of Embellishments or Grace-notes (the Turn, Trill, Appoggiaturas, Mordent, etc.), are based upon the association or alternation of a Principal tone with one or another of its Neighboring tones, thus :

Fig. 102.

" o signifies ' Neighboring note.' "

Exercises.

Construct illustrations of the above.

Organ-Point.

322.   An Organ-Point, or Pedal-Point, occurs when a note in the Bass is sustained through a succession of chords in the higher parts, part of which chords only are in harmony with the Bass note.

Fig. 103.

Notice that the chords marked × do not harmonize with the Bass, but, alternating as they do with chords of which the Bass note is a part, the effect is still good.

Essentials of Correct Organ-Point.

(*a.*)   The first and last of the series of chords should harmonize with the sustained note.

(*b.*)   The first chord should be heard upon an accented beat.

(*c.*)   Chords harmonizing with the sustained note should predominate, though they may occupy either accented or unaccented beats.

(*d.*)   As a rule, the Organ-Point is on either the Tonic or the Dominant.

The lowest part above the Organ-Point may be looked upon as forming an independent Bass for the upper parts, although the figuring is reckoned from the Organ-Point if that is the lowest note present.

Inverted Pedal, or Sustained Note.

323. When a sustained note, similar to the above, is found in one of the upper parts, it is called a Sustained Note (or Inverted Pedal). Its treatment is quite similar to that of the Organ Point.

Fig. 104.

324.   Exercises.

General Recapitulation.

325. In looking back over the last two chapters, it will be seen that the various ornamental devices employed produce dissonances, though of a passing or transitory nature. The notes which produce these dissonances do not belong to the chord, i. e., they are *not Essential* notes.

Comparing these notes with the notes which produce the dissonances in the Chords of the Seventh and other similar chords, we find that in the latter the dissonant notes belong to the chord, i. e., they *are essential* notes.

Essential notes are those *belonging to a chord;* i. e., not transitory or ornamental.

Unessential notes are those notes used with a chord but *not belonging to it.* Changing-notes, Appoggiaturas, Turns, Trills, and other ornaments are formed by employing Unessential notes.

This leads us to divide Dissonances into two classes:— those produced by Essential notes; and those produced by Unessential notes.

Dissonances formed by Essential notes are called Essential Dissonances.

Dissonances formed by Unessential notes are called Unessential Dissonances.

Essential Dissonances may be further divided into Fundamental dissonances, or those formed like Nature's Chord; and Non-Fundamental Dissonances, or those not formed like Nature's chord; e. g., Secondary Sevenths, etc.

Essential Dissonances, especially the Fundamental Dissonances, resolve naturally according to the Cadencing resolution.

Unessential Dissonances are free in their resolution or are controlled by the Melodic Tendencies of the individual tones.

The pupil is now prepared to understand the following.

Division of Chords into Three Classes.

326.   Chords are divided into Consonances, or Independent Chords, and Dissonances, or Dependent Chords.

Dissonances are divided into Essential Dissonances, and Unessential Dissonances, as explained above.

Essential Dissonances are divided again into Fundamental, and Non-Fundamental Dissonances.

The above might be shown by a tabulated synopsis.

327. Chords.

- **Consonances.**
  - Major Triads.
  - Minor Triads.
- **Dissonances.**
  - **Essential.**
    - **Fundamental.**
      - Diminished Triads.
      - Dominant seventh-chords.
      - Diminished seventh-chords.
      - Minor ninth-chords.
      - Major ninth-chords.
      - Attendant chords.
        - (The natural resolution of these chords is to the triad a 4th higher. Occasionally they progress by a False Cadence to other chords, but the unnatural effect of most of these false cadences only serves to prove the principle.)
    - **Non-fundamental.**
      - Secondary seventh- and ninth-chords.*
  - **Unessential.**
    - Altered chords.
    - Suspensions.**
    - Passing-notes.
    - Anticipations.
    - Retardations.
    - Appoggiaturas.
    - Trills, Turns, etc.
      - (The resolution of these chords depends upon the Melodic Tendencies of the individual tones.)

---

* It is scarcely necessary to class these Secondary chords separately from the Fundamental dissonances, since they usually resolve in the same way to the triad a 4th higher.

** Although the resolution of Suspensions may not seem, at first sight, to be dependent upon the Melodic tendencies of the single tones, yet when we consider that the natural tendency of one tone toward its place in the next chord has been checked, and brought into the foreground, it is clear that the melodic tendency is *even stronger* than in other cases.

From the above it is clear that all the chords used in Music may be divided into three classes: Consonances, Essential Dissonances, and Unessential Dissonances.

The Consonances are governed by the simple principles of chord-connection and part-leading; the Essential Dissonances are governed by the simple principles of the Natural Resolution of Dissonant Intervals; and the Unessential Dissonances are governed by the simple principles of Melodic tendencies, or surrounding circumstances.

Synopsis.

Write as usual.

CHAPTER XVI.

MISCELLANEOUS OBSERVATIONS: CROSS RELATION: THE TRITONE: THE GREAT STAFF: NAMING THE OCTAVES: LICENSES: SEQUENCE.

Cross Relation.

328. Any tone in a chord may be succeeded in the next chord by the same tone altered by an accidental. But, unless the same part takes both tones (the natural and the altered), there is said to be a Cross relation often producing an unpleasant effect. The unpleasant effect in cross relation is caused by the fact that these two tones (the natural and the altered) suggest two different keys at nearly the same instant, thus producing a contradiction. The bad effect can be avoided by producing both tones in the same part, giving the effect of *progression* rather than contradiction.

Fig. 105.

The above-mentioned rule, of keeping both tones in the same part, might well be counted among the Influences, since, like all other definite rules in Harmony, it is occasionally broken. For instance, in a modulation, there *are* two keys in close succession, and thus there is no contradiction.

Even where there is no modulation, the rule is sometimes disregarded, if thereby a better leading of the parts can be secured. Other exceptions allowed are Chromatic passing-notes (since the structural purity is not affected) ; Appoggiaturas (for the same reason) ; and notes which are variable, as the 6th and 7th degree in the Minor scale. (See Grove's Dictionary, Vol. I, p. 501.) These (apparent) exceptions are allowed, since the contradictory effect is less marked than in other cases, or is entirely absent.

NOTE. When the note to be chromatically altered is *doubled* in the first chord, it is obvious that only *one* of these two notes should be altered, since consecutive 8ves would occur if the rule were applied to both notes ; e. g.,

The Tritone.

329. When a part ascends by an interval of three whole steps, it makes an unmelodic progression called the Tritone (literally, "three-tone"). This can occur only in passing from the 4th to the 7th degree of the scale (unless an accidental is used). It forms an interval of an augmented 4th. The upward progression of any augmented interval is rather awkward, and this is particularly bad because the Leading-tone (or Sensitive note, as the French call it) is implicated. Although not absolutely prohibited, the Tritone should not be used without some very good reason.

The Chord of the Six-Four.

330. The chord of the $\frac{6}{4}$, although it is an inversion of the independent triad, does not give a feeling of repose, especially when succeeding a dependent chord; e. g.,

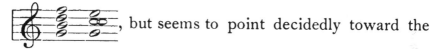, but seems to point decidedly toward the

end of a musical thought. For this reason, while well adapted to introduce a Cadencing Close, it should be used with care in the middle of a phrase. Under the conditions mentioned below it does not point so clearly to a close, and therefore may be used at any time :—

(*a.*) In connection with chords on the same Bass note; e. g., Fig. 106, (*a*).

(*b.*) In connection with chords on the same root; e. g., Fig. 106, (*b*).

(*c.*) In connection with chords on neighboring Bass notes; e. g., Fig. 106, (*c*).

(*d.*) When it is a Passing-chord; e. g., Fig. 106, (*d*).

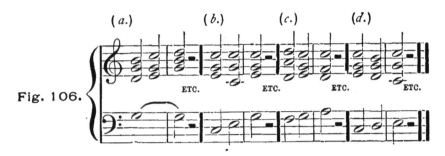

Fig. 106.

Licenses.

Advanced Course.

331. Liberties are sometimes taken with the interval of the 7th in chords of the seventh, which, though considered as exceptions, are rather confirmations than contradictions of the law of resolutions.

There are—

(*a.*) Delayed resolutions of the 7th : Where one or more chords are interpolated between the chord of the seventh and its resolution, in which interpolated chords the dissonant 7th appears as a consonance. The resolution of the 7th must, however, ultimately occur. E. g., Fig. 107, (*a*):

Fig. 107.

(*b.*) Transference : Where the dissonant 7th is transferred to another part and there resolved. It will be observed that the resolution still takes place, though in another part. E. g., Fig. 107, (*b*).

Regular Course.

Sequences.

332. A Sequence is a repetition of a progression. The progression (i. e., a succession of two or more chords) is repeated in gradually ascending or descending succession ; e. g.,

(*a.*) (*b.*) (*a.*) (*b.*)   (*a.*) (*b.*)   (*a.*) (*b.*)

Fig. 108.

In this example, the Bass alternately descends a 4th and ascends a 2nd.

To harmonize a Sequence, the parts should move so that the Sequence may be preserved in the chords and in the movement of all the parts. Thus, if in the first or " pattern "-progression the Soprano of the first chord is (for example) a 10th from the Bass (see *a*, Fig 108), the interval of a 10th should be found in the 1st chord of each following progression. (See *a*, *a*, *a*, *a*, Fig. 108.) Furthermore, if in the pattern-progression the Soprano should progress one degree downward to its place in the second chord, the same movement should be found at the corresponding place in the following progressions. (See *b*, *b*, *b*, Fig. 108.)

To carry out a Sequence exactly, it is frequently necessary to take liberties with the rules of part-leading, tendencies, doubling, and especially the rule regarding the common connecting-note for two successive chords remaining in the same part.

Sequences may occur in progressions of triads, of chords of the seventh, or of suspensions. They may also consist of the repetition of a series of two, three, or more chords.

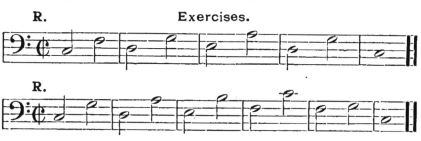

R.   Exercises.

R.

N. B.   The Tritone is here allowed, for otherwise
the sequence would be broken.

Advanced Course.   [Quoted from Banister's " Music."]

333. "A Sequence is termed Real when all the chords, or intervals,
are major, minor, etc., at each recurrence of the pattern-progression as
at the original occurrence of it.

"A Sequence is termed Tonal when the chord or intervals, at each
recurrence, are according to the key in which the passage occurs, and
therefore do not strictly resemble the original pattern.   This is the
more frequent kind of sequence.   Fig. 109 is a Tonal sequence ; two
of the ascending 2nds are major, one (from D to Eb) minor; more-
over, some of the chords are major, others minor.

" The preservation of a sequential progression, will often lead to
and justify exceptional intervals, doublings, etc.; the symmetry of the
sequence outweighing the objections which might otherwise lie against
such exceptional arrangements.   Design, using the word in its artistic
sense of intelligent aim at a defined and desirable effect, especially
with regard to form, reconciles and more than reconciles the mind to

details which, taken by themselves, would be questionable or even positively objectionable.

"In Fig. 110, for example, the Tritone 4th in the Bass, from C to F♯, and the non-resolution of the Diminished 5th in the Tenor, at ✳, till the next chord but one, are both justified by the sequential form of the passage.

"Such exceptional progressions, however, though permissible

BANISTER.

Fig. 109.

in the course of the sequence, must not occur in the original pattern, in which the writing must be perfectly pure."

BANISTER.

Fig. 110.

Related Keys.

334. In § 32 the keys related to a given key were stated to be the key having one more sharp (its Dominant), and the key having one less (the Subdominant). To these may be added the Relative Minors of the key itself, of its Dominant, and of its Subdominant. Thus the relative keys of the key of C are: the key of G (the Dominant), the key of F (the Subdominant); the key of A minor (Relative Minor of C), the key of E minor

(Relative Minor of G), and D minor (Relative Minor of F).

The related keys of a Minor key are the Minor keys of its Dominant and Subdominant, and the relative Majors of all three, i. e., of the key itself, of its Dominant, and of its Subdominant. Thus, the related keys of C minor are G minor and F minor, E♭ major, B♭ major, and A♭ major.

Naming the Octaves.

335. Musicians speak of Three-lined A, Great-octave B, Small-octave F, etc. The system of naming the various octaves is as follows :—

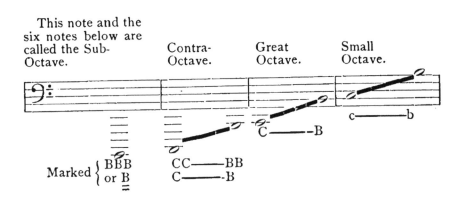

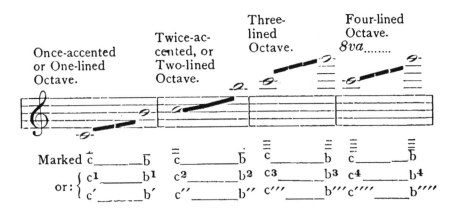

The Great Staff: the C Clefs.

336. In very old music, instead of two staves of five lines each and an added line above the Bass or below the Treble for middle C, a great staff of eleven lines was used; and the various parts, Bass, Tenor, Alto, and Soprano, were placed high or low upon this staff, according to the pitch of the voice:

Fig. 111.

The notes in the great staff were written just as in the present system, G being the lowest note in the Bass, and leading up step by step to the 5th treble line, which is F. Notice that the 6th line is C, corresponding to our middle C. In fact, our staff is the same as the old one, except that to help the eye the middle line is omitted unless actually in use, when it is written as an added line, and the two sections are separated a little.

The sign ⊞ is called the C clef, and always denotes middle C, or the 6th line of the great staff. In forming a Tenor staff, for example, it is considered in which part of the great staff the chief notes of the Tenor lie (all staves consisting of five lines and four spaces). Now, the Tenor sings most easily from the 3rd line of the great staff to the seventh line, or from small D to one-lined E. It not being necessary to employ all of the Great staff for the limited compass of the Tenor, it became customary to take out the proper section of the great staff, leaving the clef to denote which part had been taken. Reference to Fig. 112, (*a*), and 112, (*b*), will make it clear how the Tenor, Alto and Soprano staves were formed.

The C clef, then, instead of moving about for the different staves, in reality remains stationary, different parts of the great staff being used with it to suit the compass of the different voices.

Fig. 112, *a.*

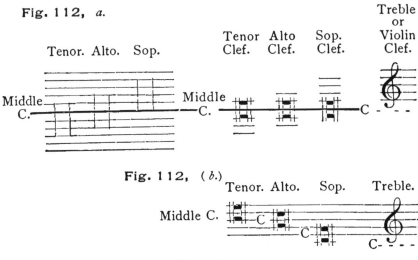

Fig. 112, (*b.*)

Exercises.

These clefs should be brought into use, either by writing future exercises in them, or by copying past exercises, hymn-tunes, etc., employing a separate staff for each part, thus forming what is called Vocal Score.

Chords of the Eleventh and of the Thirteenth.

337. According to the principle of forming chords by the addition of a note a 3rd above the last note, we may form chords of the 11th by the addition of a note to the

Chord of the 9th; e. g., ; and if to this Chord of

the 11th we add still another 3rd, we shall have a Chord

of the 13th; e. g., .

These chords have no practical application in Harmony, since so many notes must be omitted in four-part writing, and the dissonant intervals prepared, that they become practically nothing more than suspensions.

Exercises in Open Position, or Dispersed Harmony.

338. The pupil is now sufficiently experienced to write in Open position, placing the Tenor part upon the Bass staff. It is not required that every chord shall be in open position; when more convenient, close position may be used.

In distributing the parts, try to keep the larger intervals between the lower parts. Avoid, if possible, having more than an octave between the Tenor and Alto, or between the Alto and Soprano.

Exercises.

Refer to the exercises in the preceding chapters, and, ignoring the figure over the first Bass note (i. e., trying various positions), write them in Open position. The results will not always be satisfactory, but the comparison of the effect in the various positions will be helpful.

Five, Six, Seven, and Eight-Part Harmony.

339. Having studied the *principles* of Harmony rather than a series of set rules, the pupil will be able to write in more than four parts, without special directions. The Tendencies and Influences will need to be interpreted with rather more freedom, on account of the increased complication resulting from the larger number of parts.

Exercises.

The pupil will attempt to compose phrases of eight measures, introducing five, six, seven or eight parts.

CHAPTER XVII.

HARMONIZING MELODIES.

340. The pupil has learned to build chords upon a given Bass, and to connect them. It is now necessary to find appropriate harmonies for a given melody, or to supply the remaining parts for a given Tenor or Alto. Hitherto the chords have been chosen for the pupil; now he must choose them for himself. Especial care is required in this, one of the practical applications of the previous study.

The pupil has used chords in their various inversions. He has also learned that any particular note may belong to several chords, a fact which renders the first attempts somewhat confusing. For example, the note C may belong to any one of the following chords:—C–E–G, F–A–C, A–C–E, D–F–A–C, or F–A–C–E, all of which are strictly in the key of C, besides the list of altered, diminished, and [A] chords. The best harmony for a given note will depend principally upon the chords preceding and following. In the exercises below, the appropriate harmony will be indicated.

Exercises.

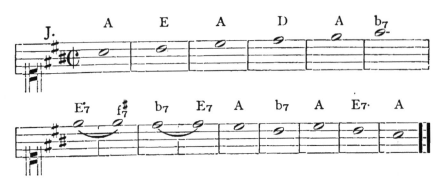

341. In the following exercises, the melody to be harmonized (also called the Cantus Firmus) is placed in the Alto, the parts to be supplied being the Soprano, Tenor and Bass.   Write the exercises in Open position.

In the next exercise, the Cantus Firmus is in the Tenor.   Supply the other parts, writing in Open position.

342. In the following exercises, in which no assistance is given, the pupil should endeavor to find chords which progress smoothly from one to another, constantly looking ahead to see if the following chord will easily succeed the one under consideration. The following hints will be found helpful :—

(1.) Use simple harmonies. Do not attempt to be original at first, but be content with commonplace effects.

(2.) The Principal triads are used more than the others, but the Secondary triads should not be neglected.

(3.) Inversions are conducive to smooth progressions.

(4.)   Contrary motion is like oil, — it helps the smooth running of the parts.

(5.)   Do not let too many parts skip at one time.

(6.)   Avoid consecutives :—not only 5ths and 8ves, but also 4ths, 2nds and 7ths.

(7.)   Keep the parts at about an equal distance from each other.

(8.)   Do not let any part exceed the limits of a good voice of corresponding pitch.

(9.)   Use the $\frac{6}{4}$ chord in the middle of an exercise with caution.   This chord usually indicates a close too keenly for use except in a cadence, or under special conditions.

(10.)   Secondary chords of the seventh resolve, like the chord of the dominant, most naturally to the triad a 4th higher.

(11.)   Apply the principles of Influences and Tendencies.

(12.)   When the Soprano is low, the chords should be in close position.   With a high Soprano, the chords should be in open position.

Exercises.

Dr. CROFT.

WARSAW.   L. M.

Other chorals and slow hymn-tunes should be selected and used as melodies for harmonization. They may be used in the Alto or Tenor as a Cantus Firmus, when transposed to a key suitable for the voice which is to take them.

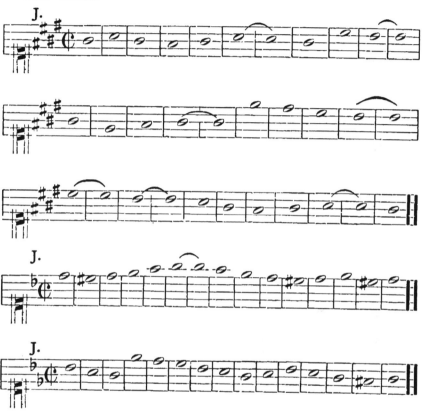

343. An interesting form of exercise in harmonizing melodies is the Chant. Being one of the shorter forms, it will be easy for the pupil to compose little melodies in the form of a chant, and then add the other parts as in the previous exercises.

The chant in its simplest form consists of four parts: (1) The first Reciting-note; (2) A short Cadence of two measures; (3) The second Reciting-note; (4) A fuller Cadence of three measures.

The Reciting-notes, or Recitatives, are so named because théy have no definite duration, but must be held till a certain number of syllables, sometimes few and sometimes many, have been sung.

The first cadence is called the Mediation. The second cadence is called the Cadence.

There should be no mark of rhythm in a chant, owing to the variations in the length of the recitative. Both the Mediation and the Cadence should be in strict time, however.

Fig. 113.

Reciting-note. Mediation. Reciting-note. Cadence.

A Double chant is, in form, like two single chants in succession, with suitable harmonic connection.

Exercises.

Form the melodies of single chants, and harmonize them.

NOTE I. It is still better to think both the melody and its appropriate harmony together, as all musicians do, on account of the harmonic connections, or the relations of the chords to each other.

NOTE II. (From Banister's " Music.")

344. " In commencing an exercise in which the melody is not given, observe the early progression of the Bass. If it ascends, be careful not to begin with the parts so near to it as to force too much similar motion. If, on the other hand, the Bass descends, begin sufficiently near it to prevent the parts becoming too much separated from it.

" In all cases, throughout the exercises, look forward, endeavoring to trace the consequences of each position and progression, as much as possible."

The above, with slight modification of the terms to make it generally applicable, forms excellent advice for this period, when the pupil makes his first attempts in independent writing.

345. If the pupil can now compose little melodies of four or eight measures, hymn-tunes, or chants, it will be of great assistance. As he will need help in regard to the formation of phrases, periods, sections, whole and half-cadences, etc., it is well to take some standard hymn-tune or short melody, and carefully analyze it, to find the number of measures in each phrase, and trace the cadences and modulations; then try to form a new melody after the pattern of the model.

To Acquire Speed in Writing.

346. In order to gain facility and ease of expression, it is well to apply speed-tests in writing exercises. To do this, review the exercises in the earlier chapters, allowing the shortest possible time for each exercise.

Practical Application of Studies in Harmony.

347. The true student will not fail to make practical application of all the subjects developed in the pages of this book. The exercises are designed to cultivate not merely a theoretical but a practical working knowledge of the chords. But in regard to proficiency in Modulating, in the use of Sequences, Passing and Changing-notes, Suspensions, Anticipations, Retardations and Attendant chords, while instruction must lead, it cannot do the work. Every one must strive for himself, not only to understand these things, but to introduce them into his productions. He should be able to modulate correctly and without hesitation, and to introduce suspensions, passing-notes, sequences, etc., into his improvisations in a natural and finished manner. This proficiency is indispensable for composers and organists, and is necessary for all who would have a broad and thorough knowledge of Music.

For this reason, the course in Harmony should not

be considered completed until several months have been devoted to the study of the subjects here mentioned, and the power of easy manipulation gained. It is not sufficient to *know* about these things; we must *do* them.

To gain this proficiency, the pupil must work for himself, under the eye of the teacher. Exercises cannot be given, as everything must be evolved from the brain of the pupil if he would gain complete independence. But the following is given to secure systematic application.

Order of Study.

348. A practical order of study in undertaking the above will be : —

Freedom in the use of the following; (1) Secondary Triads in Major: (2) Secondary Triads in Minor: (3) Secondary Chords of the 7th, including the Preparation of the dissonant notes: (4) Chords of the 9th, with Preparation: (5) Chords of the Diminished 7th: (6) Chords of the Augmented 6th in the three forms, on the Dominant Root, also on the Supertonic Root: (7) Altered Chords: (8) Attendant Chords: (9) Modulation: (10) Passing-Notes: (11) Changing-Notes: (12) Suspensions: (13) Retardations: (14) Anticipations: (15) Sequences: (16) Trills with various endings: (17) Turns: (18) Mordents: (19) Appoggiaturas: (20) Use of the Old clefs.

How to Study the Above.

(a.) *First Step: Take one subject at a time,* and, practising systematically through all the keys, form examples in connection with a suitable preceding chord (a proper introduction) and a suitable chord to follow (a proper continuation). Do not try at this period to produce a complete musical thought (pupils frequently make the mistake of attempting so much that the immediate object is lost to view), but simply learn the use of the particular subject under consideration.

(*b.*)   These studies should be made both at the key-board and in writing.

(*c.*)   Analyze examples from standard writers. Examine all music with which you come in contact, look-ing for instances of the points which you desire to learn, and noticing their treatment.

(*d.*) . Persist in practising each subject till its use becomes thoroughly familiar.

(*e.*)   *2nd Step:* Compose complete phrases con-taining illustrations of the point under consideration.

(*f.*)   Improvise short phrases, containing the de sired points.

(*g.*)   *3rd Step:* Take two subjects and try to intro-duce them alternately, or as they suggest themselves.

(*h.*)   The pupil is warned against allowing too much outside matter to enter into these improvisations, for if he wanders in search of effect of any kind, he at once forgets the object of the study, viz., to gain such control as will enable him to introduce at will the various subjects studied.

349.   It will be found that after thorough study of this branch of Harmony, the command of the chords and their connections, and of the means of giving variety, will be greatly increased.   And at the same time the musical thoughts will flow more freely, because the power of expression has been developed.

After composing phrases as above, the pupil will naturally attempt to construct little pieces, by uniting several phrases.   For this he will need special guidance, which is supplied in the chapter on Form.   (See § 359, *et seq.*)

CHAPTER XVIII.

ANALYSIS AND FORM.

350. In a work like the present it will be impossible to give more than a mere introduction and general outline of the subject, leaving matters of detail to books which are devoted exclusively to this department of musical study.

Analysis means taking apart or dissecting, and is the opposite of Synthesis, which means putting together or constructing.

In considering the structure of a composition, or analyzing it, it is natural that it should first be divided into its two or three main portions, these portions being afterward taken up, one at a time, and subdivided and examined till all the details of construction are clear.

Each of the different Movements of a composition (for example, a Sonata), is considered as a complete structure; but all are related to each other by the succession of keys and by the relationship of the musical thoughts in each. The work of the Analyst is, then, to take a complete movement and show its component parts and details of construction.

351. The basis of consideration in tracing the larger divisions of a movement is, primarily, the Theme and the different ways of repeating it. The first thing is, then to understand something of the Theme.

The Theme, or Subject, is like the text of a sermon; we do not expect to hear it (the text) constantly repeated, but it is given out or announced at the beginning; is often explained, bit by bit; is considered from different points of view; and at the close there is a sort of recapitulation or review. So with the Theme. After it is announced other matter is introduced, enlarging upon it, as it were. Next, it may appear in little pieces, called Motives, which are worked out, giving unity as well as variety. Of course, a number of keys are introduced, but they are usually related to one another very closely. How to find the Theme will be shown in § 354, where further particulars and an illustration will be found.

Form.

352. Form relates to the manner or order of introducing the various keys, the number of subjects, the manner of their repetition, etc.,— in other words, the *design* in constructing. There are various forms, such as the Sonata-Form, the Rondo-Form, the Dance-Form, the Primary Form, or Song-Form, etc. These forms vary in their design as above mentioned.

The Sonata-Form.

The Sonata-Form being a standard, and affording proper material for analysis, will be considered first. The Sonata-Form does not relate to the Sonata as a whole, but merely to the first movement. The other movements are usually written in the Rondo-, Song-, or Primary Form. The first movement of a Sonata will therefore be considered.

Two Subjects :—In the Sonata-Form two subjects, or themes, are found. One is in the key of the Tonic (the original key of the piece), and the other in the key of the Dominant.

Three Divisions :— There are usually three divisions in the movement. They are distinguished by the grouping of the keys and themes. The treatment of the two themes, the order of the keys, and the three divisions, are shown in the subjoined synopsis.

353.　　　　**Synopsis of Sonata-Form.**

I.	Key of Tonic: 1st Theme.	
II.	Connecting-Passage, modulating to	First Part. Is usually followed by double bar.
III.	2nd Theme, in key of Dominant.	
IV.	Supplementary matter and Codetta.	
V	Development, or Free Fantasia, using short motives from either theme, and passing through various keys without much restriction, leading back to key of Tonic.	Second Part. Not followed by a double bar.
VI.	Repetition of 1st Theme in original key.	
VII.	Connecting-Passage, not modulating.	
VIII.	2nd Theme, not in the Dominant key, as before, but in the Tonic.	Third Part.
IX.	Supplementary matter.	
X.	Closing Passage, or Coda.	

N. B.　There are many modifications of the above, which cannot be described in this sketch, but the pupil should attempt to note and describe them.

Application.

354.　The pupil should now take some examples, and try to locate the various points mentioned above. It will be easy to find the Development if the double bar is present, likewise the modulatory passage and the key of the Dominant; also where the third part begins with the return to the key of the Tonic. (The pupil may now try to find these points in various examples.)

How to find the Theme :—In Sonatas of simple construction, the Theme usually begins with the first measure of the composition, unless a short introduction is given, which introduction is easily discovered by its character. It is more difficult to find the exact close of the Theme without special investigation, as shown below.

The Theme should be more or less complete in itself. This does not imply that a full close should mark the end : on the contrary, the last note of the theme can be, and often is, the first note of a supplementary section or of the modulating passage.

(*a.*) If the original key is not soon restored after a modulation, but goes on into the key proper for the 2nd theme, we may know that the 1st theme has ceased, and that the modulatory passage has begun.*

(*b.*) There is no definite standard for the length of the Theme. It may be of four measures, and it may be of fifty; it may have repetitions and modulations (short ones only) ; or half-closes and other irregular features, which are at first confusing. Therefore, the best way to get the first impression is to watch the modulations, and note whether they return to the tonic key or lead on to the key of the 2nd theme.

(*c.*) Compare that which is thought to be the theme with the recapitulation, i. e., VI of the synopsis. If the two coincide, the pupil may be sure that he has found the theme. NOTE. By comparison of the theme

---

* A change of key often occurs without any indication in the signature. Therefore, the pupil must carefully observe the chords themselves, watching the accidentals and all Chords of the Seventh.

In studying the chords, be careful to exclude all Passing and Auxiliary notes from consideration.

with its repetition, the exact ending of the theme may be found; for only so much as is a part of the theme proper is repeated in the recapitulation. Where the repetition digresses from the exact notation of the first presentation, usually marks approximately the end of the theme proper. (There may be exceptions to this rule, as there are to most rules, but it will prove a valuable guide in the majority of cases.)

To trace the 2nd Theme· — It usually begins soon after the modulation to the Dominant key is established. But, to be sure of its exact beginning and ending, compare with the recapitulation. That which was in the key of the Dominant should be, at the repetition, in the key of the Tonic.

When the pupil can distinguish the boundaries of the first and second subjects, the development, the modulatory passages connecting the different parts, and the repetitions of the themes, as outlined above, it will not be difficult to recognize the supplementary matter and closing passages or coda, for they would be contained in the matter not already classified.

As mentioned before, there will be many modifications of these features, some of them occasionally being omitted entirely, and the order of keys and the arrangement of the matter being sometimes very different from the order here indicated. But in this chapter it is possible to treat only of the standard form, leaving all exceptions to works devoted entirely to this subject.

355. It will be well to begin by analyzing a Sonatina (a little sonata), as the construction is more simple and the various parts more definitely indicated than in the Sonata.

Owing to the limited space between the staves, it is

necessary to use abbreviations to mark the themes, con-
necting-passages, etc. The following are suggested and
used in referring to the different parts :—

1st Theme, I. T.; Connecting-Passage, C. P.; 2nd
Theme, II. T.; Supplementary Matter, S. M.; Coda, C.;
Development, D.; Half-Close, ½ Cl.; etc.

Before beginning the analysis, the measures should
be numbered for reference. The beginning of the 1st
and 2nd themes should be marked first, leaving the close
of the themes to be decided when the C. P., S. M., and C.
are found.

Exercises.

Taking in turn the sonatinas indicated below, the
pupil will find and mark the various points outlined in
the synopsis, in the following order:— I: III: V: II:
IV: VI: VII: IX: X. (See synopsis, § 353.)

Or I: VI: III: VIII: II: VII: V: IX: X,
tracing them in pairs as indicated by the brackets. For
example, taking the Sonatina, Op. 49, No. 2, by Beethoven.

{ I begins at measure 1 (ends at meas. 8).
{ VI begins at measure 67 (ends at meas. 74).
{ III begins at measure 20 (ends at meas. 38).
{ VIII begins at measure 87 (ends at meas. 105).
{ II begins at measure 8.
{ VII begins at measure 74.
V begins at measure 53.
IX begins at measure 105.
X begins at measure 116.

The sonatinas to be analyzed are :—

Clementi, Op. 36, No 1. (N. B. The C. P. is
short; modulation effect-
ed by a Half-Close.)

Clementi, Op. 36, No 2.

Clementi, Op. 36, No 3.
Clementi, Op. 36, No 4.
Clementi, Op. 36, No 5.
Clementi, Op, 36, No 6.
Kuhlau, Op. 20, No. 1.   (C. P. omitted.)
Kuhlau, Op. 20, No. 2.   (Development is a free ren-
                              dering of I. T., which is
                              therefore not given again
                              in the Recapitulation.)

Kuhlau, Op. 20, No. 3.
Kuhlau, Op. 55, No. 1.   (Short C. P., one mea-
                              sure only.)

Kuhlau, Op. 55, No. 2.   (C. P. omitted; mod. by
                              $\frac{1}{2}$ Cl.)

Haydn, Sonatina in C.
Mozart, Sonata in C.   (Irregular repetition of
                              I. T. in the Sub-Dom.
                              instead of Tonic.)

Beethoven, Sonata Op. 49, No. 1.   (See 1st Note
                              below. In the Reca-
                              pitulation the I. T. is in
                              left hand.)

NOTE. If a Sonata is written (i. e., begins) in a minor key, the second subject is usually in the parallel major key rather than in the Dominant.

NOTE. All the above-mentioned Sonatas and Sonatinas may be found in the " Sonatina Album, " Vol. 51 of Schirmer's Library, in an inexpensive and compact form.

Harmonic Analysis.

356. The analysis of the Form has been shown above. As soon as the form is outlined in any of the above examples, the pupil should turn his attention to the *harmonic* construction. Each chord should be marked according

to the degree of the scale upon which it is founded (simply mark them as required in previous chapters) ; the chords should be figured, attendant chords indicated, modulating chords marked by the letter showing the new key, and all Passing and Auxiliary notes distinguished from the essential notes of the chord.

Rondo-Form.

357. In § 352 it was stated that Form relates to the manner of introducing different keys, and of treating the subjects, repetitions, etc. In the Rondo-Form we may expect to find a different design from that shown in the Sonata-Form.

A chief characteristic of the Rondo-Form is the frequent recurrence of the Subject or principal theme. Another characteristic is the freedom of the order in which the different keys succeed each other. In the simplest form (there are several varieties of the Rondo) there is but one subject, which is repeated several times, an interlude occurring after each presentation of the theme. Variety is imparted, (1) by allowing the' interludes to digress into various keys (often a different key for each interlude), and (2) by the varying treatment of the theme in the repetitions.

In the more elaborate forms of the Rondo there are two, three, or more themes, and the requisite interludes (also called *episodes*).

For examples of the Rondo, see the movements marked " Rondo " in the list mentioned in § 355.

Also Beethoven, Sonata Op. 2, A maj., *Largo.*

Beethoven, Symphony No. 5, *Andante.*

Beethoven, Sonata, Op. 10, No. 3, *Rondo.*

Exercises.

358. Taking the examples mentioned above, indicate

the principal subjects, mark the keys in which the epi
sodes are written, and try and discover if there is a second
(also third) subject.   Also mark the chords.

The Primary Form.

This form, though simpler than either of those already
shown, cannot well be explained without a digression, as
follows :—

Definitions.

359.   *A Phrase:*— is a more or less complete musical
thought.   Its distinguishing characteristic is the presence
of a cadence to complete it.   The cadence need not be a
perfect one, a cadence of any sort being sufficient.

Phrases are usually of two,* four, or eight measures,
though they may be of three, five, six, seven, or other
odd number of measures.

A Period: — is the next larger division, and is
formed from two Phrases, each phrase of course having
its own cadence.   It is required that the two phrases
shall bear a certain relation to each other, the second appearing as a sequel to the first, responding to or completing it.   When the two phrases stand in this relation to
each other, the first is called the Thesis (Proposition,
or Question), and the second phrase is called the Antithesis (Conclusion, or Answer).   The first phrase should
suggest or lead toward the second; therefore, it should
not be complete in itself either with regard to the melody
or harmony — (should not end with a perfect cadence).
The second phrase, which completes the Period, may end
with a more pronounced Close.   As phrases vary in the

---

* A Phrase of two measures is technically called a *Section.* Four-measure
phrases are usually chosen to form the Thesis or Antithesis of a Period, though
there may be two Sections in such a Thesis or Antithesis.

number of measures, the Periods, being formed by the union of two phrases, will vary also.

A Motive :— is a germ of thought, which is capable of elaboration. It usually consists of but a very few notes, which have a distinct rhythmic or melodic effect. These fragments of thought are repeated in different ways and elaborated until they constitute a large part of the material. Some compositions are largely developed from motives, others from more independent melodies.

To illustrate the above definitions, turn to Kuhlau, Sonatina Op. 20, No. 1.

The *Phrase* is shown in the first four measures (also in each succeeding division of four measures).

The *Period* is shown in the first eight measures (also in the second eight).

The *Motive* is shown in the first three notes (a rhythmic motive, consisting of a dotted sixteenth-note followed by a thirty-second).

The Primary Form. Also called Liedform, or Song-Form.

360. When two eight-measure Periods a.e used in conjunction, they form, under a certain condition, a **small Two-part Primary Form.** The condition is, that the periods shall stand in the mutual relation of Thesis and Antithesis, or Question and Answer. Thus we have the principle of Thesis and Antithesis illustrated not only in the construction of each Period, but also in the relation of the Periods to each other. To comply with this condition, it is necessary to have the Antithesis of the second Period similar to the Antithesis of the first Period, though the Thesis of the second period may differ from the Thesis of the first period. For example, see Kuhlau, Op. 55, No. 2, *Cantabile.* Here the Antithesis of the second Period

cannot be exactly like that of the first Period, since the first closes in the Dominant, while the movement (of which the second Antithesis is the close) must end in the key in which it began.

Many Folk-Songs, Hymn-tunes, and simple songs are written in this form.

361.   Where the two Periods do not stand in the Relation of Thesis and Antithesis, they do not form the Primary Form, but simply a Double Period, or Period-Form. There are various forms of cadences found in the phrases of the Primary Form, but a discussion of them would extend beyond the limits of this volume.   In addition to the Two-Part Primary Form just described, there are the **Three-Part Primary Form**, produced by interpolating a new part between the two periods of the Two-Part Form (for example, see Beethoven, Op. 49, No. 2, *Tempo di Minuetto.*   The new part extends from the 8th to the 12th measure) ; and the **Large Primary Form**, produced by employing phrases of eight measures, producing sixteen-measure Periods.   Phrases may also be extended, abbreviated, or may overlap.

Exercises.

Refer to the examples given in § 355, and try to analyze the themes, marking the phrases, periods, and motives; trying to discover the relation of Thesis and Antithesis in the phrases and Periods, thus forming Period and Primary Forms where possible.

Comparison of the Preceding.

With reference to the preceding, it should be noticed that the Theme is the means by which the Sonata and the Rondo-Forms are judged; while the Phrase is the basis for analyzing the Period-form and the Primary form.

Of course, the Theme of the Sonata and Rondo may be analyzed to show their construction,— whether in the Period or Primary Form, if either. The Period and the Primary Forms may be said to represent the different methods of *construction* or of putting the phrases together, i. e., the details of the composition ; while the Sonata and the Rondo are concerned with the arrangement of the larger portions thus produced.

A succession of Phrases without relation to each other produces a Fantasia. When the Phrases are related to each other as Thesis and Antithesis, a Period is produced : when the successive Periods are not related to each other (Thesis and Antithesis), they produce Period-Form. When the Periods are related to each other (Thesis and Antithesis), they produce Primary Form.

In addition to the examples mentioned in § 355, the pupil should analyze a number of Piano-Studies or Etudes, which are usually written in the Liedform.

It will also be well to analyze the Sonatas of Mozart and Haydn before attempting those of Beethoven, which are more complex and obscure.

The pupil may now be encouraged to compose Hymn-tunes, Songs Without Words, and other little pieces, taking some standard work as his model as to length of themes, variety of keys, etc. Further instruction in regard to Form may be found in " Musical Form," Bussler-Cornell, N. Y.: G. Schirmer.

If the pupil, through his studies in Harmony, has become able, and through this little introduction to Musical Analysis has become sufficiently interested in the construction of Music, to continue his investigations in the realm of Art, the purpose of this elementary work will have been attained.

ALPHABETICAL INDEX.
